PIKE FISHING

The Practice and the Passion

PIKE FISHING

The Practice and the Passion

Mick Brown

The Crowood Press

First published in 1993 by
The Crowood Press Ltd
Ramsbury, Marlborough
Wiltshire SN8 2HR

This impression 2001

British Library Cataloguing-in-Publication Data

A catalogue record for this book is available from the British Library.

ISBN 1 85223 731 7

Dedication
To Stephanie, the best friend I ever had.

Acknowledgements
I should like to acknowledge in particular, the help I have had in producing this book from two fellow pike enthusiasts: to Mick Rouse, in conjunction with *Angling Times,* for producing the cover silhouette and most of the professional-quality, black-and-white and colour photographs, and to Andy Pearson for his excellent drawings. The excellent diagrams were produced by P Groombridge. Thanks too, to all those that I have fished with, too numerous to mention, and also to the pike anglers of the past and present whose writings have inspired me and led me to immeasurable pleasure in search of pike and pike-fishing adventures.

Those that work for the good of angling and the protection of the environment receive my respect and thanks. Without the work of the officials and members of bodies like the Pike Anglers' Club, the National Association of Specialist Anglers and the Anglers' Co-operative Association we would still be living in the Dark Ages, and anglers like myself would not have the opportunities that are now possible.

Special thanks go to my father and late mother for their long term support and encouragement and to my children Daniel and Nicola for their bravery in difficult times.

Designed and typeset by
D & N Publishing
DTP & Editorial Services
The Old Surgery
Lambourn
Berkshire RG16 7NR

Phototypeset by FIDO Imagesetting, Witney, Oxfordshire.

Printed and bound in Great Britain by
Bookcraft (Bath) Ltd, Midsomer Norton, Somerset

CONTENTS

INTRODUCTION

Pike fishing provides anglers with a wonderful opportunity to enter a magical world of escapism that is both physically and mentally demanding. It requires full use of body and mind if carried out in a determined and dedicated manner. The waterways of this country are well-endowed with these awesome predators and there are widespread opportunities for exciting, arm-arching sport. Pike fishing is more than just a sport however and the interest goes far beyond simply 'reeling them in'.

The purpose of this book is to introduce the reader to this most practical and thought-provoking pastime that has led men, like myself, to devote their whole being to its pursuit. Armed with the knowledge and advice that I am about to present to you, there is no reason why you too should not share the pleasures that I have enjoyed, provided, of course, that you are prepared to put in a similar amount of effort. The very fact that you have picked up this book and started to read suggests, to me, that there is something deep within you that is stirred by the very mention of this fascinating fish. I invite you now to enter the world of one who has spent the best years of his life in the happy pursuit of this ruthless hunter, ambusher and scavenger.

Pike fishing is not simply a pleasant way of passing one's leisure hours. If only it could be like that, if only it could be that simple! That is how it all starts, but, if you are not careful, you will be drawn deeper and deeper under its spell until it becomes a way of life for you as it has for me. Locating and catching these razor-toothed killing machines can eventually occupy your every thought until you become as hopelessly trapped as the heroin addict! You have been warned.

In order to convey my feelings for pike and detail my approach for catching them, I have tried to put myself in the position of anglers just starting out, as I did many years ago. I have asked anglers about the sort of book they want to read and can refer to time and time again. Many do not like the text book approach, as they find it rather dry and uninspiring. They tell me that they want a book they can relate to and not the exaggerated tales of heroics performed by superstars. As someone who is no more than a very enthusiastic pike angler, I have tried to give them what they want and emphasize the thought behind my fishing rather than what I caught.

At the same time I am concerned with the need for accuracy in my writing. This book is a truthful account of what pike fishing has done for me and what it has done *to* me. I hope to provide a balance of instruction, entertainment and inspiration. No attempts have been made to make the subject something that it is not. It is very much a practical book based entirely on my own thoughts and experience and not hearsay, and my observations may not correspond with those of others. No attempts have been made to bring my writing into line with popular thinking.

I offer a brief summary of my background in order to illustrate that my advice is soundly based on wide experience. I have no delusions of grandeur for I have only achieved what one would have expected from pursuing a subject for so long and I am only one of many qualified to write about it. We all tend to be individual in our approach, however, and our stories are very diverse so there is room for every man to tell his tale.

My pike fishing started way back in the mid-1960s in a very modest way as I was born in the suburbs of South Birmingham which is, as I have since discovered, just about as bad a start as a pike angler can get. Had I been born in the Fens, Broadland, near a major river, or in an area rich in mature pits, things could have taken off at a much earlier stage. No matter, I got there in the end and anyway, pleasure is often heightened by a degree of struggle.

I did have some contact with pike in my early years. In fact, I probably encountered a pike at an earlier age than anyone, although I was not conscious of the fact at the time! On the cold October morning that I was born, my father had been out piking on the Warwickshire Avon, but not for sport as we do today. In those bleak days, not long after the end of the Second World War, a pike was simply a free meal and when food was rationed I suspect that the pike population took a real hammering. That particular morning, my father came in and dropped a 7lb pike alongside me as I lay wrapped in blankets on the kitchen table, not yet a couple of hours old. Discussion then ensued regarding which was the best specimen! There we lay side by side, two of nature's most efficient and ruthless predators, one whose life had just ended and one whose life was just beginning. A strange start in life to say the least!

As a teenager, my casual interest in fishing intensified and eventually I developed a desire to specialize in catching big fish. This was a widespread movement in those days, and I feel fortunate to have been involved in one of the earliest of the specimen groups, the South Staffordshire Specimen Group, which was spawned by the writings of the inspirational anglers of the era. Although I enjoyed fishing for all species then, as I do today, I felt very much that fishing for predators was my forte. It is fair to say that big eels were my first love and this put me firmly into the category of 'eccentric'. Little has changed to this day! When the group folded, I was pleased to walk away holding the prized group predator records. My best eel was 5lb 8oz, way ahead of any other eels caught by group members.

The record that I really wanted, though, was the pike. When I joined the group, this stood as 20lb 2oz and was held for several years by Des Morgan with a magnificent Horsey Mere fish

from the sixties. Most anglers did not talk about tallies of 'twenties' in those days. In my area, it was a matter of whether you actually knew of anyone who had caught or even seen a twenty. How times have changed. I have since caught as many as thirteen 'twenties' in a season! Just before the original group was disbanded, in 1972, I topped the group pike record with a belter of 20lb 8oz, taken on a herring from a churning pool on the Hampshire Avon. Much beer was drunk that January night in the bar of the New Queen Inn at Sopley where I was staying, a scene no doubt repeated many times since, in many a bar, by many an angler!

Since that day I have added more than ninety pike over 20lb to my log book from over thirty different waters. Eleven of these weighed over thirty pounds. These are the ones that fill the magazines and impress people but the real experience that built up my knowledge of pike fishing must surely have come from more than 5,000 other smaller pike. The big ones are simply the icing on the cake. These captures came from many rivers, broads, drains, lochs, reservoirs, pits and stillwaters from all parts of the UK. Throughout the book, some of the most interesting captures will be described in some detail.

Much of my early inspiration was drawn from the writings of others. Initially, it was Bob Reynolds and Fred Wagstaff and the late Bill Keal writing in the monthlies. Then came the book that influenced many of today's successful pike anglers. When *Fishing for Big Pike* by Barrie Rickards and Ray Webb was published, my interest really took off and it was at that time that I was drawn, like so many other Midland anglers, to fish the Fen drains and rivers. Today, some twenty years later, I now live on the South Lincolnshire Fens for no other reason than to be surrounded by good pike fishing!

It never even entered my head in those days that I would one day actually be writing my own book on pike fishing. I hope that my writing will inspire others to persevere with their fishing. Everything that I can think of that will guide the reader towards rewarding pike fishing has been included. No 'secrets' have been missed out for

Two predators!

there are none. I want to save you the heartache of doing the wrong things at the wrong time, persuade you not to spend a disproportionate amount of time on insignificant actions and point out the danger of becoming a 'busy fool'.

It is important to believe that you too can emulate the captures of the so-called 'superstars' of the angling world. Determination and effort based on sound theory are required though and that means getting out on the bank and in the boat, getting experience behind you and building on it. There are no short cuts! If you are not careful, you may become an armchair angler and spend more time reading and talking about piking than actually getting out there in all weather conditions and learning first hand. There is no substitute for it. Never fear though, for I guarantee that if you are enthusiastic enough, you will succeed. I have always felt that success is 70 per cent effort and hard work, 20 per cent knowledge and learning, and 10 per cent luck.

One thing that you will not find much reference to in this book are such related topics as the biology of the pike and the history of pike fishing. This is very much a practical book. It is based entirely on my own experience. I have no intention of repeating information that has been well-chronicled elsewhere or touching on subjects which I am not qualified to write about. Much of what has been written by some authors might suggest to a beginner that one needs to be a scientist, a technician and a historian to properly understand pike and pike fishing. This is, in part, true of course, but it is not absolutely necessary in order to catch pike. Whilst the academic approach is vital for the advancement of our knowledge of the subject it is not at all necessary for the ordinary pike angler to take an interest in it if he does not want to. The basic mechanics of pike fishing are quite simple. The pike is a very unsophisticated fish obeying natural and basic instincts. Anglers who pursue them should never forget this. One hardly needs to apply space-age technology to catch them, yet anyone just starting to fish for pike would be forgiven for thinking otherwise after an initial visit to a specialist tackle shop. We use the latest equipment and theory because it allows us to be more efficient and it adds elements of interest and pleasure that were unavailable to our predecessors. Make use of them, if you can, but do not become overconcerned with advanced thinking and techniques until you have fully mastered basic principles.

Many anglers use only simple tackle and rely largely on instinct and gut feelings, and it is quite possible for them to be just as successful as those who employ a studious high-tech approach. I like to compromise. Although I see myself as a practical pike angler I realize that, to some extent, my actions are influenced by the learnings of others. Before this starts to sound rather serious, I must not forget to add that, above all, pike fishing is very good fun! You are free to choose where you fit in. Pike fish for fun or simply to relax if you wish but be aware that you are in danger of being drawn in deeper and deeper as it can be a most absorbing subject.

Newcomers are entering pike fishing all the time and I hope that they will benefit from this book. Twenty-five years on, it is difficult to see piking again through the eyes of a beginner and there is a danger that much of the content will, at this stage, go over your head. If that is the case, you should get best value for your money as this book will be of long-term value to you while your skills develop and you can later appreciate more fully the points I will be making.

I get a lot of pleasure from helping other anglers to catch fish and in particular to catch pike. My reasons for this are, I suppose, to some extent a little selfish, but I think you will agree that they are quite sensible. Educating other potential pike anglers ensures that the sport that I love is not ruined. Pike are so easy to damage. They are like small children and need protecting from naive actions such as swallowing baited hooks. As with all fish, it is easy to cause damage to them by mishandling too. It takes a long time to gain the confidence and skill to deal with pike of any size. Learning the correct way to do it, right from the start, will vastly reduce the amount of damage caused. This, of course, means that, in the long term, there will be more pike for us all to fish for and they will be in nice condition too.

Man is a hunter – it's in his nature.

There is nothing more disappointing than to slip the net under a big pike after a good fight, only to find that the previous captor has dropped it and it is badly scarred as a result.

Many times I have gone to the assistance of clumsy, uneducated anglers with a gut-hooked pike, who have no forceps. The trouble is that not everyone reads the monthly magazines and is aware of the correct tackle and procedures to use. It is second nature for me, because my life revolves around pike fishing, but some of these people go fishing only half a dozen times each season and often rely on unsound advice passed on from others who know even less than they do. When I start talking to these anglers, I see myself of yesteryear and remember the mystique of the pike and the catching of them. These are the anglers one can really help and, in doing so, help the pike themselves. Sometimes, I have come across anglers who do not want to listen to reasonable persuasion. It is a fact that you cannot hold a proper discussion with ignorant people and they have to be dealt with in other ways, but this is not the place to mention the techniques that I employ!

This book is laid out on a month-by-month basis. No longer are pike considered to be a winter-only species. This notion was proved to be rather nonsensical many years ago. The pike's condition and sporting qualities vary during the year and I have tried to capture the essence of pike fishing during each month. Of course, this book can be no more than a reflection of my own experience and can never be a complete guide to piking everywhere. There is, and I hope there always will be, much more to do! In fact, there is so much more to do that neither I nor any other individual could hope to do it all thoroughly. This pleases me in that there will always be new horizons right up until the day I finally hang up my rods.

Each chapter needs careful reading and not skimming through if any benefit beyond entertainment is to be obtained from the book in general. In the telling of tales about pike, the little things that matter will come out. The accumulation of these details helps to build one's overall ability as a pike angler.

Knowledge and practical skills, as important as they are, need to be combined with a vital ingredient that is lacking in many pike anglers. This is determination, the force that keeps the top pike men going when others give up and drop by the wayside. Confidence is also important. There is nothing like that warm inner feeling that comes from knowing that you can tackle pike in any situation that presents itself. I sincerely hope that it comes to you too some day.

1 APRIL – LOOKING FORWARD, GLANCING BACK

April has never been synonymous with pike fishing in this country so why start at this point in the year? Well, while there is still a widespread close-season, this will always be the month when the pike angler is forced to pause for a while as his opportunities to fish are considerably reduced. That's not a bad thing: apart from giving the pike a chance to rest, it also gives the pike fisherman time to gather his thoughts and take a well-earned break himself.

The piker can reflect on how the last season went and on the lessons learned. Tackle can be checked, repaired and replaced, and plans can be laid for the future. The really keen piker, though, cannot afford to wait for the close-season to arrive before tidying up his tackle. He is doing these things all the time. If he were to wait until the close-season to make repairs or purchase new items, his fishing would suffer badly. When you are obsessed with something, you simply do not let this happen. I would rather go without food for a couple of days than fish for big pike knowing that my line was suspect and needed replacing! Confused priorities maybe, but I tend to find that my life runs more smoothly when I follow my heart rather than my head.

Pike grow fat on an abundance of trout.

April is a time when more than day-to-day running repairs are required because it follows the period when I put in my maximum piking effort. I fish for pike all the year round but my favourite time is the period from just after Christmas through to mid-March. There are two main reasons for this. Firstly, only really keen anglers will be about and that means having a lot more bank space to myself. Secondly, many anglers do not realize how good piking can be during the cold-weather period. Location is an important factor, and if you get that wrong you would be forgiven for thinking that you have been wasting your time. However, this is the time of year when it is possible to find huge concentrations of pike gathered together, and some big hauls and big individual pike are on the cards. That is why my tackle is in one hell of a state by now, and a greater than usual effort is required to sort it out during April.

TACKLE OVERVIEW

At this stage it might not be a bad idea to give an overview of the sort of tackle that a pike enthusiast like me might own. I am sure that it could be very confusing for a beginner so I shall start by presenting a general picture and then fill in the detail when necessary in later chapters.

Basics Items

Rods	Floats	Seats
Reels	Weights	Clothing
Line	Hook sharpening stone	Torch
Wire traces	Bait needle	Rucksack
Treble hooks	Bait bins	Polaroids
Wire	Freezer box	Towel
Swivels	Cool bag	First-aid kit
Forceps	Rod rests	Toilet paper
Drop-off bobbins	Radio	Sharp knife
Wire cutters	Electronic run alarms	Tape measure
Scales	Unhooking mat	Fine string
Weighing sling	Holdall	Air pump
Stop-knot material	Umbrella	Ice packs
Small screwdriver	Buoyancy inserts	Chair

Additional Items for Boat Fishing

Boat!	Motor battery
Oars	Fuel can
Anchors	Motor tools and spares
Rowlocks	Ropes
Petrol motor	Carpet/Padding
Electric trolling motor	Echo sounder/Locator
Life jacket	Bailing can
Sponge	Seat

Additional Items for Lure Fishing

Lure boxes	Snap swivels
Lures	Pliers
Hook protectors	Traces
Fine emery cloth	

Photographic Equipment

Cameras	Tripod
Flash gun	Remote shutter release
Films	

This list is far from exhaustive and is simply meant to give the beginner an idea of the range of equipment required to take part in most aspects of pike fishing. It is not gathered overnight and is usually put together during years of trial and error to find what suits you and the ways that you fish for pike.

BUYING BASIC TACKLE

Your first purchases when taking up pike fishing will probably be rods and reels. How many you buy depends upon how keen you are and the range of pike fishing that you are likely to be involved in. Your financial situation has some bearing on the matter too! Legislation allows the use of only two rods in most areas but this appears to be widely ignored and many anglers use three (or more!). Take into account the fact that you might later decide to buy rods for specific purposes such a lure fishing, and you could end up, as many do, with a garage full of tackle if you are not careful. I have tried to reduce the number of different types of rod that I use myself and there is a lot of sense in choosing a good-quality, mid-range rod that will cover most eventualities. The same applies to a lesser extent with reels, and always remember that the rod and reel should go together as a balanced set-up.

I shall briefly describe what I am currently using. At this stage there is no need to give more than a basic description as more details will be given later where they become more relevant. These initial comments are intended purely to assist newcomers to piking to analyse their own requirements. The bulk of their early expenditure will be on these major items and it is important to get this right: using the wrong tackle for the job in hand or even having to sell it at a loss and buy again is extremely frustrating.

It is well worth while spending a little time deciding exactly what is required before rushing out to buy. The market is flooded with a vast range of tackle and it can be very confusing even for experienced anglers. Buying the wrong float is not the end of the world but to spend several hundred pounds on matching carbon rods and then to find them unsuitable would be, to most anglers, a disaster.

RODS

As someone whose aim in life is to make his rod bend as much as possible and as often as possible, I use rods that will be up to the job and also a pleasure to use. At the time of writing, I am working with a major rod manufacturer, Bruce and Walker, whose Waterwolf Predator rods I use with the confidence of knowing that the blanks have been designed and built on the expertise that has gone into game fishing rods with a worldwide reputation. Salmon in heavy Norwegian rivers test rods far better than any pike in the UK ever will! Bruce and Walker rods are built on their premises in Cambridgeshire and are not cheap, mass-produced, imported

blanks that have had rings whipped onto them as many are today. There is nothing wrong with these cheaper rods; they are simply aimed at a different market. To me Bruce and Walker rods are the best and the 12-foot, 2.5lb test curve MB2 model is one I now use for most of my piking. I wouldn't put my name on it if it were not a first-class product. Of course, everyone recommends their own products or those in which they have a financial interest but the general public are not stupid and do realize this. Herein lies a major problem for someone just entering the world of specialist angling. Who and what can you believe? Dozens of suppliers are pushing their rods at you, each claiming that his is the best value for money. A typical pike rod can cost anything from £50 to £200 so how do you decide? This largely depends I think on where and how you intend to fish and how often. In circumstances where one uses small baits, or fishes at close range or perhaps fishes only on the odd occasion and generally puts the rod under little stress, I can see no point in buying a rod with sophisticated mechanical properties. Most of the cheap, imported blanks with reasonable lined rings will be quite adequate. On the other hand, if you are regularly using biggish baits, casting to the horizon and fishing in situations where the rod becomes heavily stressed such as in dense weed or on big, heavy flowing rivers, it is worth looking more closely at the rod's specification. Just looking at the rod's finish and appearance though will not enable you to assess its strength and capabilities.

I would advise a beginner to talk to several more experienced anglers before purchasing this major item. Study the manufacturer's advertising literature carefully. Once you know exactly what you want, make sure you look out for rods in the second-hand tackle columns of the angling weeklies. There are some good bargains to be had, but always be as sure as you can that the rods are not stolen. Alternatively, buy some really cheap tackle and use it for a season so that you can then judge for yourself what constitutes a practical, value-for-money rod that suits your own particular needs.

REELS

Choosing a reel can be almost as confusing as choosing a rod, but at least you can see more or less what you are getting for your money. You have to take a rod manufacturer's word for the properties of the materials used in his rods but with reels the features that you are looking for are fairly apparent. The majority of pike anglers will opt for fixed spool reels although there is a lot to be said for choosing multipliers if you intend to specialize in boat fishing or lure fishing. Probably the most important feature of a pike reel is that the spool should take about 165 yards (150m) of 15lb breaking strain line. In the case of the fixed spool reel, the bale-arm should have an efficient roller to minimize line wear and, although not vital, the clutch system should give line smoothly when under pressure and my preference is for the rear drag type, which I find easier to adjust while playing a fish. I also like an anti-reverse lever that is quick and easy to operate should I suddenly need to backwind.

Reels that meet these criteria are fairly standard nowadays but, as with rods, prices vary considerably. I have for many years now put the Shimano GT4500 reels to extensive use and have found them first class. There are many very good reels for less than half of the price of the Shimanos that will be perfectly adequate for someone who pike fishes in moderation. One thing I cannot stress enough, though, is the difference in the pleasure obtained between playing a fish on a smooth, efficient reel and on a cheap or badly worn one. They all feel nice in the tackle shop when they are new, so get out on the bank and look at reels that have been in mud and water for twelve months.

BUYING WISELY

Tackle can be a rather dry, dull subject and it is best not to get too bogged down with highly technical discussion over the merits of various products. New products are emerging all the time and details quickly become outdated. It is far better to refer to in-depth reviews on particular products in the weekly angling papers such as *Angling Times,* or the specialist magazines such as *Coarse Fisherman* or *Improve Your Coarse Fishing,* all of which I can recommend. It is far better to check out tackle in this way first and then go to your local tackle dealer once you know what you are talking about. As far as pike tackle is concerned I would recommend buying from a specialist stockist such as Terry Eustace of Birmingham. Such stockists know what they are talking about because they are experienced pike anglers themselves. It is possible to see many of the top specialist retailers under the same roof by attending the National Association of Specialist Anglers (N.A.S.A.) annual conference which is usually held in April. Take a good look at a variety of tackle in a leisurely atmosphere, talk to the abundance of experienced anglers around you and compare specifications and prices.

Later on, when you have some experience of using rods and reels, you might become interested in the finer points, such as the relative gear ratios of reels or the mechanical properties of various carbon fibres, but these are of very limited use to beginners and may cause unnecessary confusion. This sort of information can be used later to refine your approach and make your piking more interesting. In ultra-long-range fishing, for example, you will find that high-ratio retrieve reels will get your rigs back to you far more quickly than standard types and with far less chance of snagging in weed, boulders or fallen branches.

There is a danger, if one is not careful, of attaching too much importance to technical detail and forgetting the prime considerations of location and feeding times. Owning a car-full of the latest piking gear does nothing other than make one look the part. The real business of piking is about a lot more than tackle, important as it may be for getting fish out.

APRIL OBSERVATIONS

Although my tackle needs to be sorted out thoroughly this month, I would not miss a good opportunity to fish for pike if it arose. There are, of course, ample opportunities to fish abroad at this time of year, should you have the finances and the time to allow it. My own explorations have taken me to Ireland, France and Holland but with such limitations placed on time spent there, I doubt whether my comments are of any real value at this stage. My own extensive experiences of early-spring piking are much closer to home, which is not to say that they are any less interesting and they are probably more relevant.

Many writers suggest that, as this is a period when pike are likely to be either spawning or just recovering from it, we should not put them under additional stress by fishing for them. Some writers, in defence of early-spring piking, suggest that ripe fish will have other things on their minds and will not be interested in taking baits anyway. My feelings on the matter are rather mixed, but I would certainly say that those who suggest that fish on the verge of spawning will not feed have got it wrong and I have seen much evidence to support this. A few examples might better illustrate this fact. On one of the last days of the 1991 season, I hooked a 14lb female pike on the River Folly in Cambridgeshire. As I brought it in, it was apparent that I had taken a fish that was involved in spawning as it was accompanied to the net by half a dozen male pike and it was exuding eggs from the vent. There is nothing unusual in that and I have seen it dozens of times. What was unusual on this occasion was that, as I returned her to the gin-clear shallow water, she was quickly re-joined by the males and they carried on rubbing against each other in the reedy margin as though nothing had happened!

On another occasion, I had permission to remove pike from a water in early April. Most of the females caught were fat with eggs to the point of bursting and could not be handled without spawn shooting everywhere. They were wolfing down deadbaits with gay abandon but at this point I decided to leave them alone as I feared we might lose some. It is purely academic whether they were at the exact point of spawning. More relevant was their condition which, at best, could be described as extremely delicate.

On other occasions I have had very different experiences, which proves to me that there are no hard and fast rules and only guidelines. On very many occasions at this time of year I have been most frustrated to find that pike, close to spawning, are just picking up baits and not attempting to swallow them. Much of the time these are only suspicions due to numerous dropped or missed runs but on other occasions I have actually witnessed pike doing just this in clear water. One pike, heavy with spawn in a river sidestream of a Wye tributary, held a deadbait lightly in its jaw for twenty minutes before I got fed up and pulled it away. I had seven runs that day and never landed a single fish! The only conclusion that I can draw is that if pregnant women have strange eating habits then why should not pregnant pike be the same?!

Perhaps I ought to mention here too the fact that you might one day catch a pike that has very recently spawned. They are not pleasant fish to look at or to handle, as they are very limp and flabby and you usually wish you had not caught them. As to my conclusions regarding whether to fish for them or not, I think I would advise against it. Judging by the very delicate state that many of the pike are in, even well-seasoned pikers might find it difficult to treat them with the special care that is necessary. I do not regret having taken opportunities to fish for pike at this time of year because at least I can say that my conclusions are based on practice and not theory, but much better to wait until a couple of weeks after they have spawned when you can see some real action!

Spawning is usually over by the middle of April, unless it is a very severe winter. It can often be over a lot sooner than this on the waters that I have been able to observe regularly. Once the fish have actually spawned, you may notice that they often look really tatty. It is surprising just how much they knock themselves about in this process. It is equally amazing how quickly they get themselves back into fine condition again, and there is nothing like the power of a post-spawned pike that is back in shape and feeding voraciously.

APRIL PIKING

Towards the end of April, I have had some arm-wrenching sport from pike that are in their most athletic condition of the season. You will sometimes read about pike that tail-walk and fight like crazy. Well, this is one of the times of year when it can be expected. They are now at a very low relative weight after months of carrying spawn. Water temperatures are rising and their appetites are uncontrollable. If you can find somewhere to fish, this can be piking at its very best.

Do not expect this sort of fishing to be offered to you on a plate. You have to go out and find it. Of course, many waters now have no close-season and it is possible to pike fish all the year round. I avoid such places as they are naturally popular with other anglers and this always makes piking more difficult. The best piking I have found in April has been on private waters or those with a close-season. Fishery managers can get special dispensation to manage fish stocks in the close-season and where this has been the case, I have many times offered my services and found some brilliant piking at a time when it would otherwise be limited. Much of this has been done

on trout fisheries where, in the main, the policy is to remove pike of any shape or size. Most knowledgeable pike anglers are in agreement that this is a disastrous policy to pursue. It leads to a worsening of the situation as small pike are no longer naturally controlled by big pike. The trout-fishing fraternity is very slow to accept this fact and, for a long time to come, we can expect to see pike stocks slaughtered instead of managed. I suspect at times that some managers do not have permission to remove pike at this time of year but do so anyway. I tend not to ask too many questions and get on with the fishing. In most cases, I not only enjoy it, but also obtain satisfaction in rescuing pike from a certain death if they should be caught by others.

Finding new homes for these pike, where they will be appreciated, can be quite a problem. Twenty-pounders are easy to relocate but the fact is that most pike caught in this way are under 5lb in weight; no one wants them and many have to be killed. I have the storage capacity to hold about a hundred pounds of pike until I can relocate them and they are killed only as a last resort. It would be totally irresponsible to drop them in the nearest water available just to save them. The

Hunting the hunter. Stalking a pike on a Lincolnshire pit.

predator–prey balance could easily be upset and pike would, through no fault of their own, gain a bad reputation in the water concerned. I am pleased to hear that at the time of writing, the Pike Anglers' Club are to lease and manage several of their own waters and these may become sanctuaries for unwanted pike from elsewhere. I hope there is enough room!

One year when I had a lot of pike on my hands, I had a stroke of luck when a local river was polluted by a tidal salt wash. For some reason, only the pike were killed, and that was an ideal place to relocate some lovely pike which I had rescued from a trout water after the salt water had receded. In theory, one needs a special consent from the National Rivers Authority (N.R.A.) to transfer pike in this way. I have obtained this in some instances and at other times I have used

common sense, moving pike to adjoining waters, for example. Most fishery owners have just let me get on with it so long as they can see the pike being removed.

Stalking the Hunter

Wherever I go, there always seems to be some stickler for the rules. On one particular trout water, I noticed a big pike lying under a bush taking in the warm spring sunshine which was reflecting off the gravel beneath her. The club committee had already given me permission to remove pike so I decided to go home, get some baits and catch it for them. Boy, was I excited. I had watched this pike for ages and it was clearly 20-22lb or so. I couldn't believe it when I returned with a rod and a couple of deadbaits to find it was still lying there where I had left it.

Normally, I would only have been confident on a trout water with livebaits. Deadbaits have proved to be virtually useless on most trout waters except when fished on the move, and even then the pike tend to grab them and drop them. At that time I had no access to livebaits but was not at all worried. It was a beautiful day, the sun was warm on my back and if I caught it, it would be a bonus pike that I was not expecting. The technique I used is probably not one that is associated with pike fishing, but I intended to stalk it. How often have you heard of stalking pike? Believe me, it is very easy providing you can spot one and be stealthy enough. I was more than confident, having taken fish up to 20lb 7oz like this in the past. I was going to drop the bait gently in front of the bush about a yard or so from the pike's snout and wait about ten minutes. The plan was then to move the bait so minutely that it would hardly be discernible. I was confident that the pike would shoot out and snaffle it as many a pike had done before for me. As soon as the pike grabbed the bait, I would strike immediately as the bait was rigged with two size 8 trebles which surely had to go into that enormous snout. I did not intend to give her time to eject it as trout-fed pike so often do.

The plan was looking good. I had been extremely quiet, which is vital, and had just made the twitch to the bait when a three-pounder shot from nowhere and grabbed it! The last thing I wanted to do was hook it and play it in front of the big pike, so I tightened up hoping that it would let go. The little so-and-so would not! He hung on and hung on until the water was churning and the big pike backed further under the bush. Eventually the three-pounder came off and the plan was resumed.

Some days you know will end in disaster and I knew that that big pike was destined not to be mine, for now a 3lb rainbow came tearing in from the depths and homed straight in on the bait. How it could have seen it from such a distance I do not know, but other similar experiences with rainbows have convinced me that they have incredible senses. The bait was pulled away just in time and a rather confused-looking rainbow

eventually disappeared into deep water. For the next hour I was plagued with the same 3lb pike and various rainbows, but I was really enthralled, lost in a little world all of my own. Everything wanted my bait except that big pike. On several occasions she came out from the bush, crossed the swim near the bait and disappeared again, only to return to the bush later from another angle.

I was quite happy to spend all day trying for this fish, when word got round that I was after it. The club members were quite pleased that I was trying to catch it but there is always one odd-ball, isn't there? He knew every rule in the book and let everyone know it. Before I could remove the pike, he proclaimed, I had to obtain form number something-or-other and then had to have the fish quarantined and health-certified. I would

A stalked pike of 20lb 7oz.

need written permission from someone to receive the pike at his water and should then acquire a stocking consent from the N.R.A.

In the meantime, the pike got fed up and moved away. I got fed up and went home. The other members got fed up because there was still a big pike in their favourite swim!

A couple of days later I was walking round the pit and got into conversation with one of the members who was unaware of the recent fiasco. After the usual pleasantries, he told me that he had hooked two lovely rainbows but a huge pike had grabbed them and broken his leader on both occasions. In the end he had left the swim as this pike was such a nuisance.

'Ought to be taken out,' he snarled. 'It was up in the top swim, by the big bush,' he went on.

'Oh really,' I said, trying not to laugh.

I have not seen that pike to this day, some three years later, but I am sure that it will be over 30lb now in such a heavily stocked trout water. I think I've talked myself into fishing for it again! There are not many in that water and as they are very difficult to tempt, I had missed a really good chance. This has been the pattern on many trout waters I have fished for pike and where they are well fed they can be very frustrating.

That period just after spawning is always a good time to try for them if you can. They will be feeding like crazy but unfortunately this also coincides with the time when many waters are restocked with trout and your bait may just be one of many easy meals. I always have to smile when I see them emptying tankloads of these tame trout into some fisheries during early spring. It is just when the pike need them most and at a time when they are

Polishing a spoon to give it more 'flash'.

in athletic shape to pursue them. I offer my advice, for what it's worth, but most continue just the same, which is fine by me as it makes the pike fatter and my fishing better! Actually, at the time of writing, I have finally convinced a trout syndicate that their pike stocks need managing rather than slaughtering, I have been given three pits to control where I will systematically reduce the number of pike to just a few big ones and eliminate the hordes of jacks that run riot on the water as a result of previous culling policies. In three or four years' time I should have some interesting statistics to publish.

LURES IN APRIL

After spending a whole winter fishing with multi-rod tactics and loads of gear, I find that more and more I enjoy lure fishing in April. Lure fishing can be great fun providing that you are getting plenty of takes, but it can become a little tedious when they are not having it. With pike activity being high, especially later in the month, this is the time to get on a water that has plenty of pike. I have gone to a lot of trouble to find places where I can lure fish in April. One particular trout water that I came across was screaming out to be pike-fished. It was adjacent to several waters that were well stocked with pike, and it was inevitable that pike would soon find their way into the trout pit, either by natural means or otherwise. In this case, I believe that it might have been 'otherwise' as the local anglers resented its becoming a private trout water.

I was told that the owner was a 'nasty piece of business' and is was not even worth approaching him. However, my advice is never to take any-one's word for anything: you would be surprised what you can get away with if you are crafty, but think it out well first. I did a little research and found that the owner of this water had a son who did not fish but messed around there in his boat. I approached the son first of all, knowing full well that he could not give me permission to fish. By asking the right questions I found out that the trout anglers were in fact getting a few pike prob-

lems. The next day, I smartened myself up, made sure that I prominently displayed my Anglers Co-operative Association (A.C.A.) badge and walked up to the man himself. He was an obviously well-to-do, outspoken type and I was not really sure which way the conversation would go. (Only a few days earlier I had tried to approach a similar-looking guy who saw me off his land with a shotgun and dogs!) However, as soon as I mentioned that I had been discussing the pike problem with his son, he seemed to think that I was a family acquaintance and became quite chatty. I never said otherwise and kept the conversation going until I was invited to help in controlling the pike. To cut a long story short, he was only too happy to hand over the pike culling to me and I virtually had that water to myself for over four years before it changed hands. I even had the use of the boat!

Since I had already got plenty of good piking to go at, I decided that as I was not in competition with anyone else, I would use this as my 'lure only' water. Livebaiting would have been too easy and after years and years of hunting pike I have concluded that there is much more to it than just catching them: I wanted to catch them in a particular way that would give me a lot of satisfaction. The water was ideal for lure fishing, being gin clear, rich in bottom weed and with some nice island and gravel-bar features.

For two seasons a big fish never showed and dozens of fish to low doubles were caught and removed to new homes. On a couple of occasions I had follows from pike that looked bigger than anything that I had landed and I enjoyed immensely the expectation of it all, not to mention also taking lots of perch over 2lb and plenty of rainbow, brown and brook trout. Boy, do those rainbows mess up a Big 'S'!

My first twenty from the water came, as is often the case, unexpectedly. Have you ever heard someone say, when referring to a keen angler, that he would keep on fishing even if someone had to carry him to the water? Well, I almost fell into that category one April. I had been in hospital for surgery on both legs and I could not walk. I was supposed to stay at home and do exercises a few times each day, to strengthen my legs. After three days in the house on my own, I had had enough and as I could drive, if I were careful, I decided to take a trip down the quiet back Fen road and have a look at the pit. I put a rod in, just in case! After much struggling I was by the water with the rod made up. I had already made up my mind on the way that I was going to cast in. The trouble was that I could not stand up for long and so ended up casting a lure from a sitting-down position with my legs to the side. It was very frustrating but I could do it, and I really felt for anyone who is permanently in such an unfortunate position. After several short sessions I had got it all worked out: I used the rolled-up landing net as a walking stick and my rucksack behind me as a back rest when casting.

A Lure-Caught Twenty

My big chance just appeared out of the blue. I was retrieving an 18g copper Abu spoon along a reed-fringed margin when suddenly from nowhere, a real mean-looking pike appeared. As I gingerly tried to stand so that I could watch the spoon come in close to the reeds, I was really shaken. I was staring into two cold evil eyes only a short distance from the rod tip. I had run out of line and the lure now hung still, half in and half out of the water, with the line going straight up to the rod tip. How long we stood in stalemate I don't know but it was long enough to get my legs aching. I had to do something as I could hardly balance any longer so I gave the lure the minutest movement. 'Like lightning', understates the speed with which the pike took the spoon from the surface and before I knew it I was struggling to stand up as the pike powered away, jumping clear of the water as it went, the reel clutch screaming. That's the way to catch a big pike! I cannot understand these people who just want to reel them in without a fight.

The following ten minutes are best described as a fiasco. Whether it was the difficulty in standing that caused me to lose concentration I am not sure, but after three or four minutes of a spectacular fight, she was weeded about twenty yards out. I hobbled round to the boat and paddled it across to where she was stuck. After a few anxious moments, I hand-lined her out from her refuge. With weed over her head she was easy to net - a belter of 20lb 13oz and 39 inches (100cm) long - which is just as well, for my legs were now in a terrible state and the stitches behind my knees had burst open. How would I explain this to the District Nurse on her next visit?!

A lure-caught pike of 20lb 13oz.

KEEPING RECORDS

The next few weeks had to be spent at home. As usual, I had gone too far but even at home a keen piker has ways of passing his time. There are many related pleasures that can be enjoyed when not out actually fishing. Ever since I began fishing, I have kept diaries and logbooks of all of my exploits and these regularly need updating and adding to. I have also always been an avid photographer of my catches and the large number of photographs I take usually needs organizing and cataloguing. As a result I can look back in great detail at what I have done and relive the pleasures over and over again. In the introduction, I stated that this book would be honest and accurate and my photographic and written records will ensure that this is so. I know many who keep no such records and when they come to recall events of yesteryear I know for a fact that they are mostly wrong for I also make some record of the notable catches made by others that I have witnessed. Isn't it funny how their fish always get bigger and never smaller? In the world of specialist angling, an individual's credibility depends upon truth and accuracy, and respect from one's peers becomes of great importance.

Keeping records can be very satisfying. My earliest entries were made in hard-backed notebooks but in recent years I have got right up to date and computerized them. I don't honestly know whether I have done the right thing: my head says yes but my heart says no. Those old, well-thumbed, dog-eared books have a lot of character to them; the computer files are very clinical and precise. The old books will fade in time and mistakes are messy to correct whereas the computer files can be easily updated or corrected. Whichever way you choose to do it, records grow over the years and as each season passes, they become more interesting to read. They plot more than mere statistics if you think about it. They are a record of your personal development.

I look at an entry made twenty years ago and the day comes flooding back to me. Why, oh why, did I fish with lures on that water? If only I had had the knowledge to use buoyant deadbaits! If only someone had been there to show me how. This is the learning curve of course, and an overall look at your results for the previous season is certainly worth while if you are interested in making any progress with your fishing. Apart from revelling in your successes, you can often see your mistakes and the problems in your fishing. As you make plans for the coming season, you can consider how to eliminate them.

When you fish a lot, as I do, it is rare to find time to keep making entries into a diary. It would be nice to have the time but my life isn't like that. So I make notes when I am out and store them in my study until I am ready to write them up properly. I often do this when the weather is too evil to enjoy going out piking. By the time that the close-season comes round though, there is always a lot of catching up to do and April is usually the month when everything gets tidied up.

Similarly my slide collection gets a good sort out. My collection is now so enormous that the only way to find anything is to number each slide and issue a computerized catalogue. Rather than sort through dozens of boxes, I simply spend a few minutes going through the listings. In this way, the slides also get handled less, which has to be a good thing when you are dealing with treasured possessions. For the future I shall be purchasing a Compact Disc photoplayer, which will be the medium that takes us into the next century. About a hundred photographs can be stored on a small disc and displayed in any order on a television screen.

If you are thinking of getting photographs published, as many anglers do, I would recommend that you take slides. Good quality 35mm slides are always in demand by angling publishers and it is a good way of helping to pay for what is becoming an increasingly expensive hobby. The most popular slide film, used by many angling professionals, is the Fuji 100 but the Kodak 64 is very good too. Their dense grain makes them ideal for enlarging and reproduction.

So, that is April. It may initially seem to be an uninteresting month but there's a great deal to be done if you have a mind to do it.

2 MAY – FIGHTING-MAD PIKE

If you ever get a chance to fish for pike in May, take it! This is the time of year when you will find out just what a sporting fish the pike is. The fish will have spent several lethargic months in low water temperatures and have undergone the rigours of spawning. Water temperatures are rising rapidly making their lives more pleasant and the pangs of hunger are striking after they have lost a great deal of body weight while reproducing. The prey fish are now either burdened with spawn or weak as a result of spawning and they are prime targets for hungry predators. Be there at the right time and some exciting action is on the cards. The pike's fighting capabilities are immense at this time of year. They are very different from the docile species that you casually reeled in at the end of the winter.

GROUP ACTIVITY

I have always believed that pike are not the lone hunters of popular myth, at least not all of the time. During April, you may have noted that groups of pike are still together after spawning and later on, into May, I have observed widespread group activity too. This is always something worth looking for as it means that good catches are possible for less effort if that prime consideration of location is taken into account. Maybe the only reason that the pike appear to be together in groups is because, at times, they are all after the same food source, such as shoaled fry in the autumn or, during May, prey fish massed together for spawning.

Over the years I have often witnessed the effect of numbers of pike apparently attacking shoals of prey in groups. To witness one of these mass attacks really is the stuff to make a true piker's heart pound faster. Where prey are heavily shoaled in shallow water, one is more likely to notice it. During the winter months in the backwaters of the River Severn I have seen some amazing displays and so spectacular are they at times that the sound of hundreds of leaping prey fish can be heard from several swims away. On an icy cold, flat calm morning there is nothing more inspiring to the piker than knowing, without any doubt at all, that the pike are on the move.

In May, prey fish are shoaled for spawning and the pike, as a result of generations of experience on well established waters, know exactly where they will be. It must be a real trial being a roach or bream at any time when there are predators about but at a vulnerable time such as this, it must be a nightmare. They are under threat from all sorts of fish, including eels, perch, trout and even chub, not to mention the land and airborne predators. It is a dangerous world down there and only the strongest survive. If you have ever watched cormorants or grebes attacking fish shoals, you may conclude as I have done that they work with each other in a quite organized fashion. I believe that pike do too at times and I have seen one particularly good example to suggest that this might be correct.

It happened on a May morning on a Shropshire estate lake. As I arrived at daybreak for the start of a long eel fishing session, I was confronted with a most interesting sight for seemingly every roach and rudd in the pool was gathered in a huge shoal that blackened the clear shallow water. They were trapped in a corner and could not escape for there were half a dozen sentries in the form of pike standing guard over them. Whether the pike had encountered them in the corner or had herded them there it is not clear, but certainly they had them at their mercy. The pike were facing the huge shoal and each pike was positioned as if it had its own territory. Now and again, a small group of roach would make a run for it only to be immediately attacked by one of the pike while the others held their positions. Strangely, the pike were not attacking the tightly packed shoals. They seemed to prefer to wait for the prey to make the first move. Of course, I could not resist putting a lure across them and took two of them on a small silver spoon before the party was broken up.

Post-Spawning Carnage

As interesting as the sighting of roach being surrounded by several pike was, it cannot compare with one of the most fascinating hours I have ever spent in my life. On one of my earliest spring piking trips, over twenty-five years ago, at Slapton Ley in South Devon, I was witness to absolute

carnage taking place. For those unfamiliar with the water, it is divided into two lakes, these being joined by a long, canal-sized channel. The main lake extends to several hundred acres and the other, although scores of acres in size, has very little open water. It is mainly reeded with narrow channels between the dense beds.

Fishing is allowed only in the larger lake and the other is a sanctuary for all forms of wildlife. Virtually every roach, rudd and perch in the lake heads into this part of the water during the spring for spawning. When spawning is over, thousands, possibly millions, of fish return, usually at dusk, to the larger lake. They pour out in huge black shoals over a period of several evenings and can be watched from a nearby bridge in their endless stream.

The first time I saw the pike was when I had stayed out a little later than I should have done in the boat. I was anchored up at the entrance that they would take into the larger lake. This area is

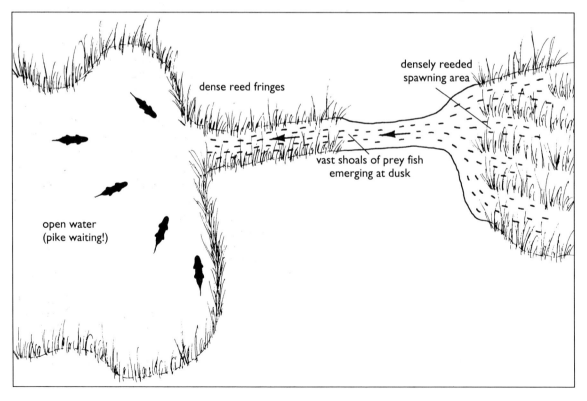

densely reeded
spawning area

dense reed fringes

vast shoals of prey fish
emerging at dusk

open water
(pike waiting!)

The Slapton 'massacre'.

massively fringed with dense reedbeds and in the daytime we would slowly drift along the margins and observe pike with their snouts just poking out and facing the open water. The only takes in daylight would come from a livebait cast right against these reeds. As it got dark, at this special time of the year, things changed very quickly. As if someone had turned on a switch, all hell would be let loose as the shoals of prey fish appeared from the channel. Maybe three or four pike would strike together and small fish would be jumping in their thousands.

In the flat calm of the evening the sound resembled someone throwing handfuls of gravel into the water. Before the water had chance to settle the next attack would begin. Livebaits and lures cast into the fray were often taken within seconds and seven or eight pike would be taken in quick succession before it was too dark to see what we were doing. As we rowed back to the mooring, pike would be striking all around us. Had the pike been of a large size we would have fished on, but, tired and hungry, we left well satisfied with the action we had had.

For me, these examples are evidence in support of my feeling that pike are more involved in group activity than we suspect. I may have it wrong of course. It may simply be that many pike in a water are after the same thing, that is the best food supply, and are acting as individuals in the same place. When the food fish are concentrated, then so are the pike. When the prey are widespread, so too are their hunters. Perhaps it only appears that they have some sort of social structure. It is only on rare occasions that I have seen anything that would go further to suggest that they do.

One memory that always sticks in my mind, another May sighting, is of two 20lb plus females casually swimming side by side in a stretch of shallow, gently flowing water on the River Wye in Herefordshire. They were probably pike that had grown up together in that part of the river, sisters perhaps, and sauntered along much like a couple of housewives strolling through a shopping centre. Perhaps they do have more than a basic

existence of eating to survive. Perhaps they even communicate in some way. Who knows?

Missed Opportunities

I have many other recollections of group activity but from the practical angling point of view it is enough to accept that this happens more than we think. The way we go about our fishing should, therefore, take this into consideration if we are going to catch more than just the occasional pike. The reason I say this is because I am convinced that so many opportunities are missed by some pikers simply because they make too much noise in landing fish. They do not realize the importance of getting a bait back into the swim as quickly and quietly as possible. Where you have just landed a pike it is quite likely that there are others nearby, possibly even swimming around with is as you play it. I have long believed this to be important but never more so than after a May session on a Staffordshire Reservoir a few seasons back. I will take you through that session now and show you what I mean. In doing so I will also describe a basic, simple rig that catches a lot of pike and than no angler who calls himself a piker should be unfamiliar with.

TROUT WATER PIKE

As with much of my spring piking, this most interesting day took place on a trout water where I had previously been allowed to fish but on a very occasional and well-supervised basis. My only piking there prior to this day had been done in cold weather and only lasted for a few hours each time. I was getting very frustrated in not being able to really get to grips with the water. Pike like these that are well fed are particularly difficult to catch and it seems to me that you can do everything correctly and still fail because they are not in need of food at most times.

The reservoir had been drained about six years earlier and yet was now repopulated with roach, perch, carp, tench and pike, plus the stocked trout. Whether someone had given the coarse fish a hand or whether the draining of the 45-acre

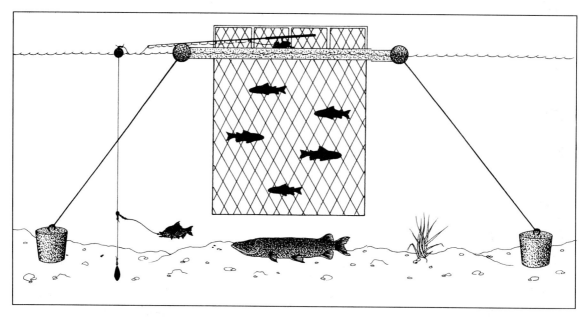

Trout water pike are attracted to the floating stock cages.

reservoir had not been done thoroughly enough, I don't know, but there were certainly plenty of fish about at this time. Small pike soon became noticed, snatching the trout anglers lures, and were removed indiscriminately by all means. I had managed to rescue some of the better fish and relocate them and was slowly gaining the confidence of the manager, Chris Buxton. He was starting to appreciate that I really was only interested in the pike and that his trout were the last thing I wanted to catch.

Eventually I became very friendly with Chris and we are good friends to this day. It is only now that I realize why trout fishery managers appear to be against us. I have found that they are completely disillusioned by the cheating antics of anglers in general. Trout anglers are no better than any others in this respect and after years and years of being ripped off, Chris was naturally very cautious. More importantly, game anglers live in a different world from their coarse fishing colleagues and do not, in most cases, understand just how seriously pike anglers in general take their fishing and how concerned we are for the fishes' welfare. This is only natural, I suppose,

when they live in a world where virtually every fish caught is bashed on the head and eaten! At this stage in the proceedings, Chris had not fully appreciated the need to manage the pike stocks properly and was bent on removing as many as possible by any means. One day he decided to organize a major pike cull for he had witnessed a sight that had disturbed him and one that I would have loved to have seen for myself.

One of Chris' interests was diving and during the warmer months he used this to his advantage for checking the condition of the nets on his floating stock cages. They were anchored out in the middle of the reservoir in over eighteen feet of water. Such was the clarity of the water at that time that you could actually see a herring lying on the bottom at that depth! As he went down to check, he was staggered by what he came face-to-face with. Hungry pike surrounded the thousands of trout enclosed in the safety of the nets. Even though pike could not get to them, they were attracting them like a magnet. Here and there the outer safety nets had been ripped by pike that could not resist attacking albeit to no avail. Altogether there were seven pike there, all quite big ones too. They appeared completely fearless and swam around him. It must have been an eerie experience.

On his return Chris declared that the pike would have to go, and the following Saturday morning would see all the people that he could trust out there in boats, armed to the teeth with rods and livebaits! This was lucky for me, for I had been invited to go along. Less lucky was the fact that my wife had to go into hospital and it was arranged for me to take the children to visit her on that day! There was just one chance though, I had a few hours free on the Wednesday morning beforehand and decided to see whether Chris would consider allowing me to go up on my own and try for them. After all he did want those pike out badly. I have always found that by asking the right questions at the right time and choosing one's words carefully, one can achieve a surprising amount. It was no problem, I was all set to go and livebaits would be laid on too!

When I arrived at the arranged time of eight o'clock, the water was flat calm and the sun was beating down. There were several trout anglers' boats out but I would be well out of their way as the area around the stock cages was out of bounds to them. If I were to tell you that these floating cage platforms were in need of a little maintenance, that would be understating the problem to a considerable degree. A death-trap would be a more adequate description! This, Chris informed me, was to make life difficult for anyone trying to steal his trout. It was certainly making life difficult for me! After two hours struggling on rotting timber, trying to drift livebaits around the area of the cages, I had seen no signs of pike at all. The only offer that I had had was from a huge trout. It inspected the bait in the gin clear water about 15 feet below the cages. As I was hoping to fish there again, I decided to pull the bait away from it! Apart from this incident, the free-swimming roach livebait had been either ignored or unseen by the pike.

I wondered whether the pike were right under the cage. As time was ticking away, I changed over to a paternoster rig which I lowered against the netting of the floating cage upon which I was

Mick Brown unhooks a 23lb 4oz trout water pike for photographer Mick Rouse while Mick gets busy with the camera. Team work aids efficiency.

standing. I was so close to the float that I could simply reach out and adjust the stop-knot so that it was set to perfect depth for it to be on the surface. There was no other acceptable method I could use for indication of a run. I estimated the gap under the cages to be about three feet and set the livebait a foot off bottom.

Expecting a long wait, I climbed into my boat, which was anchored on the other side of the cages a matter of five yards or so away. I did not fancy standing on that timber framework for much longer as it was breaking up and it was a struggle to stand there for very long. I had not even settled in the boat when the bung whacked under with a very audible 'plop' and the rod bounced as the line pulled from the elastic band on the butt. God, I live for these moments! Even after catching hundreds of good pike, the adrenalin was pumping madly as I scrambled as quietly as I could to the rod. Oh, the sheer pleasure of connecting with a big fish in such interesting circumstances!

The cages were anchored at each corner to very heavy concrete blocks on the bed of the reservoir. The danger was that the pike might snag on the anchorage ropes and had to be played in a very tight arena. At every opportunity I had to let go of the reel just to hang on a bit more tightly to the structure of the cages. The power of the pike was pulling the footwalk down and below water level. As a poor swimmer, I was getting just a little concerned! It was a good fight by any standards and an enormous pleasure to watch the fight in such clear deep water. 'Here she comes now, get the net ready.' I am talking to myself all the time like this when I am fishing, 'My God, what am I seeing, there's loads of them!' At least half a dozen pike were surfacing and the one on the end of my line was nowhere near the biggest! To have such a sight thrust unexpectedly on one is a mind-blowing experience. As the pike slipped into the net, the others dispersed, only to reappear again briefly as if wondering to where their unfortunate sister had gone.

The fish was weighed at 17lb exactly and sacked ready for transfer. People say that fishing is a good therapy for taking your mind off all your troubles and this was a case to prove it. I forgot all about Steph lying in hospital and recovering from an awful operation. All I could think of was how I was going to make the few baits I had left last for me to get a couple more fish in the net. The problem was that Chris had only six baits waiting for me when I arrived and only two of them were alive. One had just been used but luckily I got it back, albeit now badly chewed.

Sink and Draw Tactics

In order to conserve baits, I decided to use the chewed bait to sink and draw through the swim. The pike could not miss it if they were still there. This method can be really deadly and is so simple, yet it is amazing how few pikers cannot be bothered to use it and prefer to sit and wait behind static baits. Nothing could be easier to rig up and it is simply a matter of tying a two-hook trace to the line and adding the necessary swan shot to the trace near the swivel as required to get the bait to sink at the desired rate. I never pinch them, especially the modern lead-free shot, onto the line itself, for fear of weakening it. The fish is hooked with the top treble firmly in both lips and the other lightly in the flank. In this instance, as baits were scarce, I used an old dodge of tying it to the trace. I always carry a reel of fine kitchen string with me for this purpose.

Quite a long time passed but I had no response. I had tried high in the water to start with and worked progressively deeper but to no avail. It might have only been ten minutes or so but I had expected an immediate reaction. I had also kept very quiet and as well concealed as I could. It is so easy to forget these basic principles when you are not catching anything and, by sheer carelessness, miss an opportunity by scaring any fish that may come into range.

I knew that I had not been detected on this occasion. Maybe I hadn't covered them yet? I decided it was possible that they had moved well away from the cages after that little disturbance and started casting well out and all around the area. After five minutes or so I got another shock in the form of half-a-dozen big pike, several of them obviously twenties, following, inquisitively, behind the bait. There was no spectacular chasing or lunging at it. They simply inspected it from all angles as they followed, some from the sides and some from underneath. I ran out of line and so let the bait drop back into the depths close to the cage. As it did so, one showed interest and as I retrieved it again, it was taken. Just like the other one, this hooked pike was followed everywhere by the others until it was netted. At 16lb 4oz it was obviously one of the smaller ones.

After struggling on the water for each and every fish I had taken there in the past four years, I was now confronted with several pike just there for the taking. My next sink and draw bait was

Mass attack!

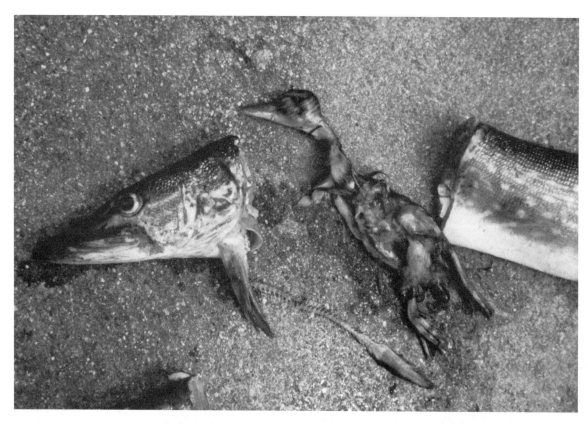

Pike will eat anything that moves, in this case a duckling and a small eel.

taken almost at the rod tip again, this time by an incredibly hard fighting pike of 22lb 6oz. At this stage, I realized that one of the others was a particularly long fish and was noticeably lighter in colour than the rest. That was the one I wanted!

Each time the pike came in to attack my sink and draw bait, the big one held back. The next bait was grabbed by another fish that was obviously well over 20lb but that one slipped the hook at the net. I had just lost a twenty and it seemed to matter little. My mind was on that big one. Several times I drew my bait away from good fish just to give the big old girl a look in. I almost felt guilty catching these pike for seeing them feeding together was a strange experience. As they twisted and turned and changed positions whilst following baits they almost seemed to be a family group working together. As they turned their heads to follow the movement of the bait, they appeared to have quizzical looks on their faces

and, when that last one had been hooked, I would swear that the others with her were enquiring whether she was all right! Perhaps they are not entirely the cold ruthless killers that we take them for and do have some degree of consciousness and feeling. Then again, perhaps I have spent too long fishing in the sun and snow even to consider such a thought!

A few frustrating minutes passed and then finally it was just me and the big one. On one retrieve she was at the head of two or three other big fish. She followed the bait very inquisitively, nudging it and inspecting it in a most peculiar manner. I ran out of line again and she just waited there under the rod tip, every detail of her massive frame visible in the bright sunshine. I kept every limb of my body still except for the minimum movement that was needed to use the reel which I pulled close to my body. I buried my chin down into my chest to make sure that the

This 22lb 6oz pike was caught during a spring cull on a trout reservoir.

reflection of the sun on my face did not frighten her. This could not be happening to me! Had she seen me? Would she panic and bolt away? I moved the bait in slow motion just beneath the surface with probably only a metre or so of line from the rod tip. My brain was nearly exploding as she sidled up to it and took it just like a dog gently taking a biscuit. The release of bodily tension when I struck was tremendous. All I had to do now was get her in the net. She had to be a thirty because of her amazing length!

Horror of horrors, I knew this day wasn't real, it had to be a nightmare! As if the pike knew exactly what to do, she swam straight through a loop in a rope connected to one of the huge concrete cage anchors. The loop was about seven or eight feet down and about 18 inches in diameter and I could not imagine ever getting that fish back again. She powered away and I back wound like crazy, the line clearly grating and chafing on the rope. Initially my heart sank, but then I had a burst of confidence. There was nothing to lose and everything to gain, I told myself. I allowed the fish to continue running to get her well away from the rope and to give me time to get into the boat and over the top of the problem.

At that very moment a slight breeze decided to get up and the water became choppy, making it awkward to hold position and see beneath the surface! The line was grating and grinding as the pike ran and ran. I was in a mess! After twenty minutes of gaining and losing line I was wondering what to do. I then had a ridiculous plan to poke the rod tip right down to the loop and keep reeling in until the pike was at the rod tip and then ease it through. It seemed a little unlikely that it would work, but what were the alternatives?

How the line held I just do not know. The abrasion on it must have been terrific. Good old Sylcast! With the boat almost capsizing and me reeling underwater the plan went into operation and with almost two yards to go the pike, unbelievably, swam back through of its own accord! I'm sure I had willed it to do so! Now I just had to play the lively beast on line that was virtually worn out. Another ten minutes passed, as I was too worried to use a lot of pressure in case the

The lines and wire I recommend for most pike fishing.

line did go. And then she was finally netted. One absolutely exhausted angler sat in the sunshine for ten minutes looking at his prize in the net and recovering!

The 44-inch fish, weighing 26lb 6oz was sacked with the others awaiting transfer. It was a tremendous fish which had without a doubt recently weighed over 30lb before spawning and, if left in that water, I have no doubt that in about four or five months' time she would have done so again. Alas, this was not to be the case, for she had a new home waiting where her future weight gain was not so certain, but at least she would be alive, and well away from the murderous hands of the trout anglers.

The next hour was spent in equal bliss when a couple of thirteens and another seventeen-pounder came to the net and then it was time to go as I had an appointment in the afternoon. The 26lb fish went into a pool that held very few other pike but good numbers of quality roach and bream. I have never fished for it again to this day even though I would have liked to monitor its progress. There is just too much to do!

Those few hours piking remain, to this day, one of my most enjoyable memories despite catching lots of much bigger pike and taking much bigger hauls. It is not what you do but the way that you do it, as the saying goes. I hope that the tale has demonstrated that it is necessary to work at a situation to get the most out of it and catch more than just the odd fish or two. Perhaps it is also a lesson in not panicking when all seems lost. I have had many pike snagged or in difficult landing situations but, with a little thought and by avoiding making hurried decisions, it is possible to get out of most of them successfully. Above all, even if you cannot see the fish, consider that they might be present in large groups and fish accordingly.

RELIABLE LINES

Using reliable tackle that you are 100 per cent confident in helps you enormously. The Sylcast line that I was using when I caught the 26lb fish was 11lb breaking strain and was chosen for its good knot strength and excellent resistance to abrasion. At the time it was the line chosen by the most discerning pike anglers and the only criticism I had was that it did not come off the spool straight, having what is known as a 'high memory', i.e. it retained its coiled form when not under tension. This led to a few tangles especially with the type of bobbins which stayed on the line during a run with a rod set on rests. While Sylcast is still an excellent line, there are now, in my opinion, some better lines on the market. The one I now use most of the time is Berkeley Big Game in 12lb breaking strain. This line actually breaks at an incredible seventeen pounds! You will cut your hands trying to pull for a break if you are not careful! It is fine in diameter and comes off the spool quite straight and limp yet has incredible abrasion resistance properties and high wet

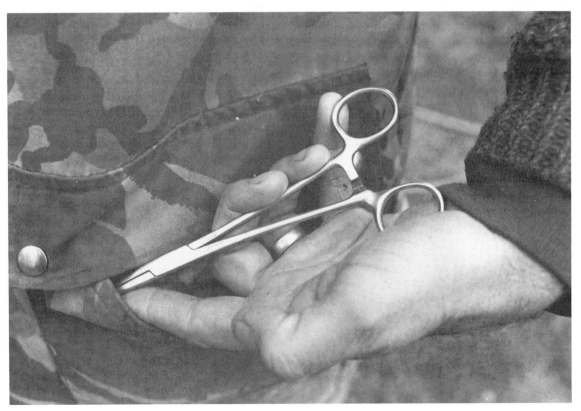

My forceps are always carried in my left-hand pocket so there is no need to rummage around for them when I need them.

knot-strength. At the time of writing, I am also using Bagley's Silver Thread AN 40 which I am finding just as good. These lines are quite pricey but do not have to be replaced so often. As line is a vital link between you and the pike, it is foolish to settle for second best.

IRISH PIKE

This time of year is a particularly good one to test line and, in fact, all tackle, to the limit, for pike fight incredibly well during the month of May. It is this exciting prospect that takes many British pike anglers across the sea to Southern Ireland during this month. Virtually everyone that samples Irish spring piking comes back with exciting tales of their arm-aching battles with lean, mean predators that spend half of their time out of the water during the fight. While this is perfectly true, I would say that some exaggeration and possibly lack of experience is shown for pike virtually anywhere fight like this in May and other warmer months. Sampling the fighting power of Irish pike is not the only reason that pikers flock there in the spring though. It is simply such a lovely place to visit and has no close-season as we have in most parts of Britain. This makes it an ideal holiday break at a time when our own pike fishing is very restricted.

The pike fishing on many Irish waters is difficult for many to get to grips with in a short holiday break. If you river fish in Ireland, you need to know a little about tackling heavy flowing, often

Playing a big pike on an Irish lough. It came off!

deep, water. If you prefer to fish stillwaters, you will, in many cases, need to be experienced with boats for many waters are difficult to fish from the banks due to extensive reed and bog fringes. The simple fact that not many anglers use these waters means that there are not many prepared swims in the boggy and swampy margins. However, should you decide to try the awe-inspiring huge loughs, you take your life into your hands for they are formidable, forbidding places to tackle.

The problems encountered on the smaller waters are not insurmountable if one uses a little common sense but the big waters are different and worth mentioning. My experiences on these big waters is very limited. Were they closer to hand things would be very different for they provide really challenging piking and the chance of a very big pike. The main thing to bear in mind on a first visit to Ireland to fish a big water is that it will not be a picnic and survival is a paramount consideration. If you think otherwise, please do not risk it. This is not intended to frighten you away from these waters but to warn you. As with any trip to far away wild places, planning and preparation will eliminate most of the nightmares that can and do happen, should you decide to go.

There are obvious considerations such as the booking of ferries and accommodation and this can become quite expensive unless you travel in numbers. Three or four people travelling and staying together reduces costs considerably. Warm, comfortable, night-time accommodation is essential - you must plan for the fact that you will probably get very cold, wet and weary. There are some very good, friendly guest houses in most areas although some anglers prefer to be independent and sleep in vans and caravanettes or even bivvy out. Whatever you do, prepare for the worst for it might well happen. Heavy winds and continual torrential rainfall are characteristic of Irish spring weather.

When you arrive in Ireland, the first thing to realize is that your time is limited. Many of the good piking marks may well involve motoring across the Lough for over an hour to reach them. It is most dangerous, in fact suicidal, to be on these waters in the dark, so the usual practice of setting out early and coming back in late is unwise. With this in mind, it pays to gather as much information about swims and locations before you go, from anglers who have been before. Save the pioneering until you know a little more about what you are doing!

Try to get someone to draw you a map of potential good areas and get as many landmark features as possible. If you have never been to Ireland it is hard to imagine the scale of the bigger waters. You will need to be guided initially by prominent features such as buildings and pylons in the general direction that you intend to fish and then, when closer, by bankside features. When you are approaching from a mile away, all the bays, promontories and inlets just appear flat. Do not to forget to know what feature to head for on the way back! It is easy to get lost on these massive expanses of water.

It sounds pretty straight forward so far, doesn't it? If the surface of the waters were flat calm, it would be. Now imagine that there is a two-foot swell on the water. That is quite ordinary on these Irish waters. It might be calm or there may be just a gentle swell when you set out but within a few minutes the water can start rolling and you can suddenly find yourself in a four- to five-foot swell and the engine propeller spends a proportion of its time out of the water as the boat dips and rolls. If you are prepared for rough weather, it is bad enough but if you are not and are a mile from shore and heading for a reef, it can be frightening. Only a fool would go out unprepared and, in fact, no good boatman would allow you to use his boats or let you go out if you looked as though you could not handle a difficult situation.

Most anglers will hire boats although there is no reason why you should not take your own if it is suitable. Suitable boats are long, usually 15 feet or more, ruggedly built and have adequate buoyancy. Life jackets should always be worn but I doubt that they will save your life if you are in the icy water for very long. The cold will kill you first but at least, as one boatman told me, they will find your body and you will get a decent burial!

Engines are always used to propel such big boats on these waters and if you take your own, make sure you are very familiar with it and carry spares and tools. I had one very frightening experience when my engine failed in a huge swell, over a mile from shore. Only my intimate knowledge of the engine allowed me to change the plug as I hung over the back of the boat which was soon hopelessly out of control. The engine started up just in the nick of time as we fast approached a reef which could have smashed the bottom out. I spent five horrific minutes hanging over the back of the rolling boat while one of my companions tried with the oars to keep us from going broadside on to the waves and the other lay flat in the bottom to lower our centre of gravity and stop us from tipping over!

When you finally arrive at a chosen secluded bay and start enjoying the fishing do not forget that you have got to get back at some time. There are several vital things to do to ensure that you

return to tell the tale. You will hopefully have had the sense to listen to the weather forecast before setting out but will need to be continually updated. I always carry a small radio with me for this purpose. Wind direction and force will dictate the course you plot back. It is not unusual to motor a mile in the opposite direction from that you wish to go in in order to avoid motoring across the waves. Make sure you have got sufficient fuel in case this happens. Also carry an Ordnance Survey map of the area with you in a plastic bag. In rough weather you may have to abandon the boat and walk, as I have done a couple of times, and it is useful to know the access to the nearest road or cottage. Do not forget to have sufficient food rations just in case you become really stranded somewhere.

Anyone who has not tackled these waters would be forgiven for thinking that I have

Big waters demand big boats.

Hand landing a small pike on a drain near Amsterdam.

exaggerated the difficulties. Anyone who has been on these nightmare waters in foul weather will not!

As for the fishing, to be honest it is largely a matter of taking into account what the pike are likely to be doing when you are there. In May visiting anglers like myself with very little knowledge of these places will head straight for the shallow weedy bays where prey fish gather to spawn.

These places are usually dry in summer but if the winter rainfall has been sufficient, these grassy, bush-strewn areas will be flooded by spring, which makes them the perfect spawning habitat.

Whether you catch will depend upon timing. Fish move in to spawn and then later move away to the deeps again. Several attempts at spawning may take place dependent upon water temperatures and different species may even spawn at different times. It is simply a matter of being there when it is all happening and you may be very, very lucky and bag up or, by doing nothing wrong, be very unlucky and catch nothing.

When the pike are feeding, bait choice may not be too critical and most anglers are quite happy with deadbaits such as mackerel, smelts and herrings. Livebaiting is not allowed in Ireland.

Pike come very close in to the shore in these bays if not disturbed and can be spotted either swimming or swirling right next to the rods. It is an advantage to take a pair of chest waders to reach fish that might be much further out as these shallow bays can be colossal, sometimes hundreds of acres in extent. In many, it is possible to wade out 40 yards in shallow water and then cast a further 60 yards away to get baits to bonus fish that others without waders cannot reach. Make sure you have got plenty of line on your spools!

Whether you sit it out in one bay and wait for the fish or try different areas is entirely up to you. That is half the fun as there is so much to explore and you can only be guided by your feelings at the time. When the water levels fall to normal in the summer and the prey fish have left the shallow spawning areas, the pike will be well-dispersed around the lough, and a completely different style of fishing for them will be required. Trolling lures or fish baits at this time is quite a specialized skill that only really experienced anglers would tackle and yet, ironically, the fairly inexperienced angler who pike fishes the spawning bays in spring can catch considerably more fish for less effort. The serious piker knows this and realizes the relative merits of each style. Should you find kind weather in May and get in amongst the pike, you will have experienced piking at its best!

The author with a 27lb 10oz pike taken on a drifted roach bait from a lough in the west of Ireland. The best fish of a trip that produced a massive haul of over 750lb.

3 JUNE – ARM-WRENCHING ACTION

Not many anglers would consider fishing for pike in June. I would not myself unless, of course, the piking was really exceptional. Much of my June piking has been tagged on to sessions after other species, but that was until I realized that there are times when it is worth going all-out for pike and with very good results.

When I fish for eels and zander at this time of year, pike are often snaffling both fish and worm baits in the middle of the night and worms soaked in pilchard oil are a real favourite. Pike are very active in the dark in June and take all sorts of baits. Many a potential big eel has turned into a pike after running off with a fish section presented sub-surface during the dark hours.

When the first few rays of light are breaking through, pike can be even more in evidence, often crashing out and disturbing the calm surface with their presence. Some June mornings they seem to snatch everything in sight when they are in this mood. They grab swim feeders, worms, boilies, leads, and floats, in fact anything that moves! Fortunately for the pike, most anglers are either unprepared for tackling them or cannot be bothered which is not a bad thing really because it takes an especially careful angler to handle them at this time of year. That is because they fight like demons in the warm water and then, if allowed, they will flap all over the place on the bank and only a confident angler would be able to deal with them properly.

When I look back at my early fishing years I realize that I missed some very good opportunities by not taking advantage of fishing for pike in June, when they were obviously feeding. On prolific pike waters such as Cheddar Reservoir or the Fenland Drains and rivers, I now know that I should have tried a little harder than slinging a plug around for an hour or so after my all-night eel and zander sessions. I should have made a little more effort to reach those reservoir pike that were chasing big roach, just out of range of the plugs, or been prepared with livebaits for those drain pike that fed briefly and fiercely at dawn. Looking back on missed opportunities is all part of the learning process though and it is no good living in regret.

Some of the best piking I ever experienced in June and the other summer months has been with river pike. This will be described in detail in the next chapter. This is really very predictable fishing and I only do it occasionally knowing that it will always be there. Good June piking is not always guaranteed though and it is often a case of keeping your eyes and ears open and looking for opportunities that come your way.

A THIRTY AT LAST!

The most memorable June piking I ever had came in just this way at Gailey Reservoir in Staffordshire. In the last chapter I described a magic day there in May. The seven pike that I caught in a few hours' fishing totalled just over 125lb and, as a condition of fishing, I had to transfer them to other waters. Not many waters can take such a loss and for the next two or three years, my occasional visits there produced very few pike, the best going to mid-doubles. I had lost my inspiration for a big pike from there. In fact I had all but given up, when suddenly events took a turn for the better.

As if from nowhere, big pike were being spotted again and what is more I now had more experience under my belt from other waters and had

Playing a summer-reservoir pike.

soon started to catch a few. One particular day will long be etched on my mind.

That glorious morning at the end of June dawned still and warm. It was as a June dawn should be as I chugged up the M6 motorway towards the reservoir in my ancient caravanette, affectionately named 'The Snail' by the kids. Having had the shock of going back to an indoor job again after a long break and now working shifts, my system was badly in need of all the fresh air and relaxation that it could get and nothing could have been better that the warm, comfortable atmosphere of that morning. The sun was well up as I waited in the car park for Chris, the manager, to arrive. Quietly and confidently I checked over every detail of my tackle. 'Nothing must be left to chance,' I kept telling myself. The last two trips across there had produced only one run each day but they were amongst the hardest

fighting pike I have ever encountered in my life. These pike were both lean and nowhere near back to their normal weight since spawning which must have been in each case well over 30lb for they weighed respectively 27lb 13oz and 28lb 1oz. Both fish were 41 inches long and clearly different fish because of their distinctive markings. Pike anglers have long established the fact that pike can be recognized in this way and recaptures can be easily proven by the trained eye.

The vivid memories of those monsters were turning over and over in my mind as I guided the ready-made-up rods through the back doors of the van. This was the ideal fishing vehicle as 12-foot rods fitted in easily without having to be taken down. Everything had to be perfect with such big pike waiting to be caught and, although I was desperate to get over the bank of the reservoir and get started, I slowly continued with my

Drifting tackle. Note: float, drilled bullet, line greaser, tub of grease and binoculars.

checking ritual. As soon as other anglers arrive and the chatter and banter starts, it is easy to miss something that might be regretted later. My favourite pair of old Terry Eustace Long Range carp rods, now in retirement, were quickly checked over. The 11lb breaking strain Sylcast line was new but examined closely over its last few yards just in case it had been damaged. As there were no weed or snags in the reservoir worth worrying about, this tackle was perfectly adequate but it can come in for some punishment if the pike decides to play games with the anchor rope. I was rigged up ready to start drifting live-baits for I had already worked out from my last two visits that this was most effective.

Before Chris arrived, I was joined by my good friend Colin Dorsett, at that time proprietor of a tackle shop in Tamworth and later to become well known around the Midlands as the Silstar agent. He had business to sort out with Chris and I hoped he would be able to join me for a few hours' piking. I should remind you that Gailey was, at that time, exclusively a trout reservoir although it held good coarse fish. Prior to this date I had been the only pike angler to obtain permission to fish there but a change of policy meant that day tickets were soon to become available. My intention on this particular trip was to try and catch a really big pike to help publicize the opening of the fishery to coarse anglers.

I had already sneaked a look at the water immediately after I had arrived. The sight that greeted me gave me a feeling that cannot really be described but I will try. The knowledge that I now had of the water and the pleasing vista that it presented to me, represented everything that the heart of this piker desired. My mind wandered for a few minutes to what I could do there, given no restrictions and no interference from anyone else. I knew that I could turn this water into one of the best pike fisheries that had ever existed. By careful management I could end up with a dozen pike all between 25 and 40lb plus and still make the water profitable as a mixed trout and coarse fishery. In the winter months, I would close the fishery and quietly fish for the pike with just a few close friends. We would break all records and tell no one ... but back to reality! What about those hordes of cormorants and that early summer algae bloom, what about poachers and ... and in any case, I have not got the money to do it!

Colin's arrival brought me back to earth. Even if I could not have my way I was not going to miss out on piking of this quality and a chance of a personal best pike. Chris then arrived and while Colin and Chris talked business, I sorted out the best boat. They were well made 12-foot wooden punts and we had to take to the oars to get us around as there were no engines but on less than 50 acres of water, on a fine summer's day this was no real hardship. The boats were very stable, in good condition and, with no recent rain, were also pleasantly dry inside. The tackle was quickly loaded and I was desperate to start fishing although trying not to show it.

With business quickly concluded, Colin managed to get permission to join me in the boat for a few hours' piking. As we rowed out to the point where all the action was taking place, I told Colin everything that had happened on the last two trips and the best way to fish it. It really was the most pleasing type of piking that I can imagine. We positioned the boat about forty yards upwind of the place where I had recently caught the two high twenties and anchored across the light south-westerly breeze so that we would both be comfortable as we fished down to the productive area. It was difficult to be very precise about the exact spot that was producing the fish but the technique that we would be using, greased-line drifted livebaits would take this into account by covering all the water in the locality. I had not got a fish locator or sounder at the time to enable me to get a good look at the reservoir bed contours,

Casting a deadbait on drifting tackle. Applying line grease to line greaser on rod in foreground.

but could see no reason at all why the pike were in this open featureless water. This is often the case and the fact should not be ignored that pike are not always located adjacent to prominent features particularly where food is abundant.

The Drifted Livebait

There are several variations on the drifted livebait technique. To cover excessive distances, usually from the bank, specially designed floats are used with large vanes to catch the wind and send the bait to the horizon. This obviously searches a lot of water. They employ special top rings that break free when striking or retrieving fast and reduce the resistance that the float would otherwise offer. Sliding weights are used on the main line to ensure that the float remains upright, even if the bait rises in the water. The best sliding leads incorporate a plastic sleeve to minimize the possibility of line wear. Distances of up to 150 yards (137m) or more can be achieved. Some anglers drift baits ever further using special large-capacity reel spools and binoculars to keep in touch with their floats. Greasing the line to make it float is essential with this technique and purpose-designed line-greasers can be used which are fitted into the butt ring. They are packed with line grease and automatically grease the line as it is pulled through by the drifting tackle. The best products of this type were developed by Eddy Turner and Vic Gibson and are available through E.T. Fishing Products.

From a boat, I prefer not to drift too far as I prefer, if possible, to make immediate contact with a pike as soon as it takes the bait. This reduces the chances of the bait being swallowed too far down the pike's throat. With not so much line out, there is less delay in contacting the pike and therefore less likelihood of it ejecting the bait. Striking at closer range should also give a better hook-hold. From the bank, it is possible to walk or run backwards to take in the excessive amount of line quickly and gain contact and control of a taking pike but obviously this is not possible from a boat and so I prefer to drift no more than about 70 yards and then reposition the boat to cover new water.

Longer drifting distances may be necessary from a boat in certain circumstances. If several boats are anchored close together in a good area it may be difficult to keep changing position and so a longer drift might be the best option. Like-wise, it may not be possible to take a boat into a restricted area such as a nature reserve, and so a long drift would be needed there too.

On this particular day, I decided to use my favourite and quite simple drifting tactics using a standard 1¼ inch drilled poly-ball as a sliding float. I had worked out the killing method for the current conditions and it had made the fishing even simpler for the pike were in the top layer of water, as I had found by catching them on my last two visits. The swim was eight to twelve feet deep yet the pike were obviously high in the water. Deep drifted baits had been ignored or unnoticed yet baits fished at only two to three feet deep had taken several fish. Also of interest was the fact that the takes were coming to quite small, four to five inch, roach and perch baits while big baits, both roach and trout, were either ignored or bothered by jacks. This, I have since learned, has been the case on similar trout waters where I would have expected the exact opposite to happen. The greasing of the line, in order to make it float, is vital to keep control of the bait and also to prevent the livebait swimming over the main line and risking a bite-off from a taking pike. A well-greased floating line catches the slightest breeze and offers very little resistance to prevent a float from drifting with it. With a little practice it is even possible to create a bow in the line on the surface to guide the float in the direction that you wish it to proceed. The method really is simplicity itself and is constantly interesting as the bait is continually covering new territory which might produce a take. On your own it is possible

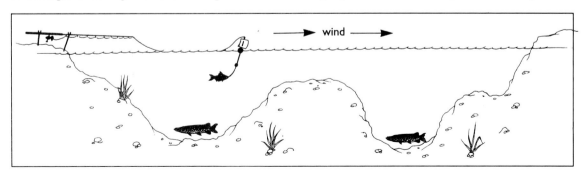

Drifting over uneven terrain the float has to be set for the shallowest point and may miss fish in deep holes. Trolling over such terrain poses similar problems.

to take control of two baits with a little care. With someone else in the boat it is best to fish just one drifter each. If you want to use a second rod, it is better to set up one with either a paternostered livebait or float fished deadbait to your own side of the boat. Keep it within easy view while you concentrate mainly on the drifter.

Colin and I were soon anchored up at Gailey Reservoir and putting this theory into practice. It is always the same when you take a friend fishing and really build up the picture of what should happen to whet his appetite. Nothing happens! You start to feel bad about it and after an hour of fruitless drifting this is exactly how I felt. The sun rose higher. We peeled off our top layers of clothing and decided this was to be another disastrous blank. Nowadays, with many more seasons under my belt, I know a lot better than to feel like that on a good water. An hour or two is nothing in the scheme of things and we had simply not put the bait in the right place yet. If the pike are on the move, and so is your bait, it is conceivable that fate might never see them converge even if they are in the same area.

At late morning, we up-anchored and moved. Looking back I don't think that that was a bad idea. It is possible to miss pike in a swim but it is just as easy to drop on one by moving to a new swim. In a water with such low pike density and with pike that are so well fed, I am convinced that you need a little luck on your side. Even if you are fishing the water properly you can miss out if luck is against you. Luck did not seem to be with us at all that day. The piking had rarely been frantic there anyway and now it was a war of attrition. The slow fishing either wore you down or you persevered until you got one. Now if the fishing is boring, it is a mindless exercise to carry on like this but that morning, to me at least, was not at all boring. The sun was hot on our backs, we had got plenty of livebaits and the water had the potential to turn up a monster. What more could we ask for? Apart from a run of course!

By mid-afternoon, Colin had to think about leaving to attend to some business. I suggested that we anchor up in our original position and drift baits for a final half hour while we finished

'Watto' took this thirty in the swim I'd decided not to fish – so close again!

our coffee and sandwiches. There we both sat on an idyllic summer's day. A run would have made it perfect. Others around us were trout fishing and hundreds of thousands of others throughout the land were bivvied out for carp and tench or trotting the rivers for chub and roach. What were these two men doing pike fishing on such an unlikely day? I did momentarily wonder myself as my eyes strained to watch the glistening lines snaking into the distance to meet two red bobbing floats. As often happens, our floats had come quite close together not far down the drift. It is funny how you always find your partner's float more interesting and while watching it, Colin's bung whacked down. What would it be? The bung was still visible; it was being held to the surface, exactly as it had been by the previous monsters. In each case they had taken the bait and remained high in the water with it. Colin was almost shaking as he wound down. After all, I had really built him up for something special. 'Oh dear', I think he said, as a three-pounder flapped on the surface all the way to the boat!

Fresh baits were put on for the final drift and, unexpectedly, we were into a repeat performance except that this time it was my bung that plopped under and was held by a pike in exactly the same way. Like Colin, I was using a lively five-inch perch and could see no need to do anything other than strike straight away. I almost felt guilty, but at the same time very pleased when I met solid resistance. It was definitely a twenty but Colin thought that I was joking when I told him so. When you are having a good time in the boat, you often do not realize when it is time to be serious for a while. Suddenly it did get serious, very serious, as the fish threw itself straight into the air and

crashed down with a hefty 'splodoosh', 'I was kidding you Col, it's not a twenty, it's a thirty,' I said, tongue in cheek and expecting it to be a mid-twenty. After all, I never catch thirties do I?

To be quite honest, I never thought much about its weight as I enjoyed the spectacular arm-wrenching scrap. It did cross my mind for a second that it might beat my current best of 28lb but I was concentrating on making sure that it ended up in the net first. We had all the usual antics as the pike tried to tangle with the anchor ropes and did its best to be as awkward as possible but, then again, who wants to reel them straight in - not me! After about five minutes of arm-aching action I was thinking about foregoing my principles after getting a good glimpse of the pike as we missed her with the net the first time. She was colossal! Next time we made sure and I, knees trembling, was suddenly pulling the mesh tight to the side of the boat so that she could not jump out.

Summer pike are long and lean and jump all over the place as this twenty-three-pounder did.

I had to decide now whether to get the fish to the bank to unhook, weigh and photograph her or do it in the boat. There are no hard and fast rules about this but the safety of the pike must come first. In a big boat with a very experienced partner, I would now opt for staying in the boat to do the job. The fish would be quickly back in the water and the chance of another big pike from the same swim could be taken. At this time, I was not so experienced as I am now, but still, I hope I did the job properly as far as the safety of the pike was concerned. With the pike lying very safely in the landing net, we gently paddled the short distance to the shore where the fishery holding tank was waiting, ready-filled with water.

At the mooring, I attempted to pass the fish up to Tim, the bailiff, so that he could put it, temporarily, in the tank. As I lifted her up to him, I knew she was the heaviest pike that I had ever caught and the figure of thirty passed through my mind but not my lips as a large crowd gathered. I sat by the tank drinking coffee for a while and my mind pondered how a relatively small, single size 6 treble could have held in those mighty scissors and hauled such a monster in. Why did she bother with a small perch when the water is stuffed with quality roach, tench and trout? I will never know, but I am glad that she did!

The fish was unblemished and not in any way distressed as it lay there. My only concern was that it should get back into the water in the same way. For this reason I never found out her true weight. The 32lb Avons bottomed out at 32lb 12oz. Two sets of scales lifting together showed a much heavier weight but I would not accept weighing a fish in that fashion as errors can creep in. After a few photographs she was gently slipped back and I settled for the minimum weight of 32lb 12oz. I did not care that she was actually heavier. I had caught a thirty, my first thirty! I might never catch one again and I was a very happy man as I prepared for the rush to get to see the family and then back to Peterborough for work.

Catching a thirty has to be a glorious, memorable occasion, but to do it in the company of good friends on a beautiful summer's day makes it very special.

THE SEARCH FOR A THIRTY

Since that day on Gailey Reservoir I have amazed even myself by catching another ten thirties. The weekly press proclaimed that, after Eddy Turner, I was the only other angler to have ever caught ten or more fish over this magical weight. As nice as it feels to have this glory thrust upon me, my feet are firmly fixed to the ground and I can see it in its true perspective. A few years previously, I did set myself a target of catching a 30lb pike, it is true. Where such an idea leads one is in the lap of the gods. Luckily, they smiled on me! Perhaps a brief resumé of how I went about achieving my ambition will offer some encouragement to others who think that they could not do it themselves. I have no special knowledge or special privileges of access to good waters. My results are based on nothing more than enthusiasm and effort. The fact that I was the only pike angler to fish Gailey Reservoir was not a privilege bestowed upon me lightly. I had to work at it as I did all the other places that did not produce a thirty.

The search for a thirty had started many years previously in the early eighties. Prior to this I was just as enthusiastic about pike fishing but my outlook was limited by lack of wide experience and contact with other anglers. I was a bit of a loner, I suppose, and was content with doing what I was doing and limiting my shared experience with a few close friends. As long as the floats kept shooting under and the bobbins kept dropping off, I didn't worry too much about how big the pike were. Each season brought good numbers of doubles and usually a twenty or two. This, in those days, represented good piking results for most of the people I knew, but here and there were anglers making the headlines with the really big pike. I looked at the results of the big names such a Nev Fickling, John Watson and Eddy Turner and what they were doing. Like me they were fishing obsessively. I knew 'Watto' very well and I knew that I caught just as many, if not more, pike than he did at times, but he had a much better record of bigger fish. John and the others would not have caught those fish that made them famous from the waters that I was on.

'It's a thirty!'

The reason was simple – the fish were not there to be caught! The top pikers were fishing waters with big fish reputations; pits, lochs and Broads.

Living in Birmingham did not help matters much either. There was one big fish in the vicinity, the 'Beast', at the Packington fishery. Each season it came out several times at over 30lb but to fish for it went against all my principles. The fact that it had been caught endless times before did not bother me. It was a magnificent fish and full credit should go to those that did catch it. To fish around a small pit though, with a dozen other anglers all after the same fish, was not my idea of interesting fishing. I went a few times and did not enjoy it. The odds against me catching it with dozens of baits out most days were enormous. I have a simple rule with my fishing – if I don't enjoy it, I don't do it! And I didn't!

In a way, the decision to stop fishing for the 'Beast' was probably a good thing as it made me

think a lot more about what I was doing and subsequently widened my pike fishing experience. My current favourite water at that time was the Severn and, be it summer or winter, I had worked out where and how to catch pike consistently and keep the rod bending. When you reach this happy state of affairs it is easy to stagnate even if you are catching many good fish. I believe that humans have an enquiring mind and an underlying urge to move forward and make progress in all things but sometimes we need a kick up the backside to get us to make a little effort.

In a hasty moment, which was painful at the time, I made a decision that I will never regret. After a very successful day in early October 1983, I thought about the future. I might go down to the river a couple of times each week and catch dozens of double-figure pike with top fish going just over twenty pounds. It would be just as I did last year, and the previous couple of years. With the best of the winter's fishing to come and having paid my mooring fee, I winched my boat from the river. It was time to break new ground!

Although I didn't realize it at the time, this was the first step along the path from being a very keen pike angler to becoming a fanatic, obsessed with but one thought — to catch huge pike. That evening I sat by the fire, planning in my mind and then on paper how I would tackle this project. With a young family to look after and at that time struggling to make a living, time would be at a premium. Time normally spent pleasure fishing would have to be foresaken. Places that did not stand a chance of producing a really big pike would have to be forgotten. Some I would really miss, but I knew that I could always go back to them, perhaps in years to come. New waters would have to be explored and I would have to find the money from somewhere to start travel-

ling longer distances a lot more regularly. Time must not be wasted on the wrong waters. The more you fish the right places, the more that the odds are stacked in your favour and it might, just might, come right one day!

A list of waters was drawn up and eventually cut down to a realistic number. The final choice consisted of three venues, each one very different to the others. The Broads was peaking at the time and thirties were making the headlines every now and again. Had I realized just how few and localized these fish were I might have foresaken the 340-mile-round trips to fish there. With the help of my friend John Watson of Norwich though, I would be well informed of where the big fish were coming from.

Next on my list was the River Wye, a beautiful river which I had known since a boy yet, in recent years, had rarely fished because of its distance from my home. Rumours were circulating that

The Wye turned up some beauties including this stocky twenty-two-pounder.

the pike fishing was taking off there, and, knowing its reputation from the past, I thought this river to be a reasonable gamble for a huge pike. The knowledge that I had from my younger days might give me a head start. In such marvellous surroundings, failure would not matter too much, though thoughts of failure never entered my mind.

Finally, I could not ignore the trout waters. The ones opened to the public did not interest me in the least prior to this. Bough Beech and Llandegfedd have since changed my mind of course! Anglers were paying a lot of money, using methods that made catching unlikely, and fishing where pike had been extensively culled. I knew that I would have to get involved eventually or I could miss out. There was also the small trout reservoir at Gailey where I had fished in the past. This too, was extensively culled but I could not ignore the fact that such a place could grow a

thirty in seven or eight years and at least I had a chance to fish it using proper tactics. I would have to make efforts to get permission to fish there again. Had I been wealthier I would have considered trips to the popular Irish and Scottish waters but as this was not the case, I had to forget them. I did eventually fish in Ireland taking pike to over 20lb but that was not what I was looking for.

The three projects, if I can call them that, were started simultaneously, and I fished all three venues as soon as any suitable opportunity arose. Other fishing was foresaken and my spare time was spent either trying to make some money to finance the trip or spent with my family to make up for time spent away from home. Not an easy balance to achieve. Hours were spent poring over Ordnance Survey maps in the evenings and my head was continually turning over ideas while I tried to concentrate on work.

A summer-caught reservoir double taken on long-range mackerel tail.

The Wye was only fished in winter when there was a drop of water in the river. In summer it can be painfully low and weedy. It is perhaps ideal for short sessions but not for someone like me having to drive a long way to fish. With immense nostalgia I explored sections of the middle and lower river, mostly alone but occasionally with friends. It was all new to them but my mind wandered to my childhood days and our large family gatherings spent camping by the river at Kerne Bridge. I remembered the huge salmon that my father and uncle used to catch there, not to mention the roach and chub. Very pleasant fishing.

The trout water was fished by occasional invitation from the manager who was a friend of my brother. The number of invitations grew as I twisted his arm a little by offering to help out where I could with fishery work. I even left my boat there so that it could be used as a hire boat. Sometimes I would spend a whole day there just to get permission to cast in for an hour or so but must admit that this made the fishing even more pleasureable. People say that anything that comes easy isn't worth having. I really believe this is true.

Finally, the Broads. What can I say about this piker's Mecca that has not already been said? If only I could have spent even more time there. Even in decline, the pike fishing is better than you will find most places elsewhere and the keen piker living there has a head start on all the rest of us. I decided to stay clear of the Thurne, where the really big pike were coming from, as I thought that my short trips would be better spent in one or two other areas that had good potential but were not under so much pressure. This is a decision that, in the light of present knowledge, I deeply regret.

Over the following seasons, the numbers of pike caught fell dramatically but I was catching much better quality fish and had got caught up on a learning curve that I had not even known about before. The piking proved to be very varied and extremely interesting. Of the three venues, the Wye was probably the most enjoyable. It was mainly one-to-one fishing, an angler with a rod searching out each swim as he came to it. The sound of the water and the gloriously mild end-of-season days will be etched on my mind forever. The 'plop' of the float and bringing heavy battling pike back against the current is an experience never to be forgotten. My best from the lower river was 22lb and from the middle river 21lb 6oz with many high doubles backing them up. The fishing was very satisfying even if I did not get the particular fish that I was after. On one occasion, a thirty was caught from the bank opposite one of my regular haunts. The swims on that bank were much better than those I was fishing. At least my theory was correct!

Broadland proved equally satisfying in terms of fun, pleasure and interest although the good catches were punctuated with blanks as we searched for fish. The fishing is not easy there by any means. Long hours were often spent just trying to find fish but when they were found there was marvellous sport to be had. It was all boat fishing, and after walking miles and miles along the steep rugged banks of the Wye, I found it refreshing to gently row or motor from swim to swim with comparative ease. My years of boat fishing on the Severn had been good preparation for this type of piking. The pike caught made up for the long distances travelled and hardships involved. I caught twenties from four different Broads and from the River Bure with a best fish of 27lb 9oz. The nearest I got to a thirty was photographing one for 'Watto', shortly after he had dropped in a swim that I had decided not to fish! So close again!

At around the same time, I was doing some part-time fishery work for a Midland netsman. One morning I called in to see what had come back from a job that I had not been on. There in the tank were several twenties and the biggest pike that I had ever seen. It was awesome! As it pulled the scales past 33lb, I knew I had to catch one like it!

Then finally there was the water where it all happened. The story has already been told but with a little luck on my side it could easily have been about one of the other venues instead. Still, when it come to pike of this size, one out of three is not bad!

4 JULY – OUT ON YOUR OWN

IN PARADISE VALLEY

Imagine how you would feel if you had just entered paradise. That might go some way towards describing the feelings that ran through me on those idyllic July mornings of yesteryear as I slipped my boat away from its mooring in a backwater of the huge and mighty tidal River Severn. The days always seemed to dawn in a cold stillness that, despite the promise of warmth to come, always made me shiver as I touched every cold and damp item. It always seemed silent there too apart from the distant background rumble of the ceaseless torrent of water pouring over the weir sill.

The river had tragically claimed several lives in years gone by and this fact was never too far from my thoughts. As a poor swimmer, I would have to be a fool to venture out there in a small boat without a life jacket. When the piking action gets hectic, it is so easy to make that one mistake that can be fatal. With this in mind, my boat had been well prepared for safety. Anywhere extra buoyancy could be added, it had been. Polystyrene blocks had been cut and wedged into every conceivable place to ensure that there was no possibility of sinking should an accident occur, especially with the heavy burden of tackle on board.

The anchors were home-made and consisted of nothing more than one-gallon paint cans filled with concrete. Metal loops were cast in position to enable a rope to be tied on. These anchors were quite heavy enough for the flow that we fished in. If the flow was such that they would not hold then it would be certain that the river would not be worth fishing anyway. The anchors are fitted on hooks outside the boat in order to give plenty of room where it is needed. The anchor ropes themselves are important and any old rope will not do. They must be strong, and nylon is much more reliable than rope made from natural fibres which can rot in time and suddenly let you down. The rope should not be too thick either as a thinner rope is easier to handle and takes up far less storage space in the bottom of the boat.

For any boat fishing, it is advisable to have decent rowlocks that are matched to the oars and do not easily pull out of their location holes. When out on a big river, this is vital as one could get into a lot of trouble if a rowlock went over the side. It is always advisable to keep a spare one stowed somewhere in the boat, just in case. Another item worth considering, which I hope you will never need, is a very sharp knife. One thing that always frightens me on the river is the thought that a huge submerged branch or part of a tree could come down the river unnoticed and tangle the anchor rope with dire consequences. I have had one or two come quite close and, believe me, it is an unnerving experience when they suddenly pop up from nowhere or scrape unseen along the underside of the boat. It sends a shiver right down your spine. At least you should be prepared to quickly cut the anchor rope if necessary.

Oars seem too obvious to mention but even these need deeper consideration for this type of fishing. Most oars will pull you across a stillwater, and generally once you get the boat moving they come under little stress. Not so the oars on the river piker's boat. Pulling up-river against a strong flow puts them under terrific strain and they must be strong enough for the job. It puts the oarsman under terrific strain too, and is certainly not an exercise for the feeble. At least you

A boat is the only way to fish a big river properly.

get an easy ride on the way back! Better to invest in a motor if you are not up to the rowing but you risk the wrath of others by disturbing the peace of the river valley unless you use an electric type. To me, boats get cluttered enough and I will only use one if really necessary.

All of this safety work is done beforehand of course, long before the boat is launched on the river. Safety has to be the prime consideration. As the boat approaches the end of the backwater and the oars feel the first pull of the current you will know that your attention to safety has not been wasted and more than one angler has admitted to being unnerved by a first encounter with the moving water. Once the haul against the current starts there is no time to stop and pause on a river; you need to know exactly where you are heading otherwise you will end up back where you started or even further downstream if you are not careful!

The first thing that the river piker must do is assess the condition and mood of the river. In time you will learn how this affects your chances. The two considerations that I am concerned with are the flow strength and colour. During the summer months, the flow varies from downright sluggishness to a frightening torrent. The ideal speed is a gentle pace which would take a trotted livebait 100 yards down river in about four or five minutes and be such that when I hold the bait back against the current it will rise slowly to mid-water. As far as colour goes, I like a light green tinge to it so that you can easily see the oars three or four feet below the surface. More coloured water does not deter river pike from feeding if they need to, but I think their vision range is reduced to the point that they do not see your bait so easily. It is worth remembering that when the water is coloured, a livelier bait will compensate for the pike's reduced vision by sending

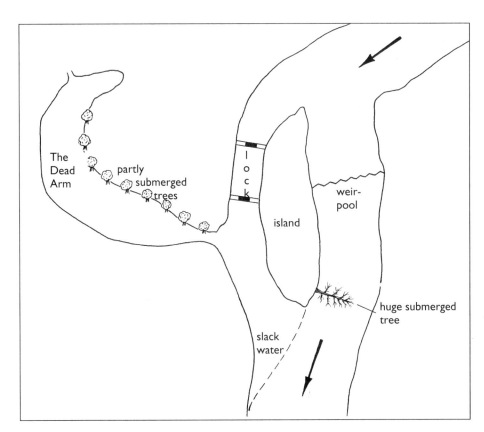

The River Severn at Tewkesbury.

stronger signals to its lateral line receptors. Strangely enough, in very clear water conditions pike do not seem to feed as well as when that slight tinge of colour is there and this may be due to the fact that the prey shoals are more wary at these times and keep well hidden as they feel vulnerable. River pike, like pike anywhere, know exactly when the optimum time to feed will be and rarely waste much energy at any other time.

Colour and flow strength, to some extent, go hand in hand. On the Severn a heavy flow usually means coloured water and that, on this river, means the colour of strong tea. Very light summer flows due to drought and heavy abstraction usually see the river with an unhealthy green colour. When it is just right it has a light-green tinge and a light, i.e. walking pace, flow. If this occurs following either of the above extreme conditions, that have slowed down pike activity for a while, things are perfect. The Severn also suffers from temperature variation due to compensation

water being released from the Welsh Reservoirs but it is debatable whether this has any great effect by the time it has reached the tidal river where I fish. However, further upstream, it might. After fishing the river in its many moods for a few seasons, patterns start to emerge. Just looking at the water conditions now gives me strong gut feelings about how the fishing will go and I'm usually not far wrong.

CATCHING LIVEBAITS

Let us consider a typical day when things are looking promising. It did not take long for me to learn that the Severn is a livebait water and the first task is to get enough baits for the session. In July it is difficult to keep baits at home so it is usual to catch them before the start of piking. Often, this can be a frustrating exercise but on the Severn it is usually no trouble at all, if you know what you are doing, of course. Many visiting pike anglers have trouble catching bait there, but I found it very easy. The reason is simple. I spent the first seven or eight years of my fishing career pleasure fishing on the Midland rivers before I became involved in specialist angling and the experience paid dividends when I needed it most. I was in a position to appreciate just how much easier it was to bag up with prey fish from a boat. A major problem when float fishing for the shoals of roach, dace and chub that inhabit the Severn is keeping a steady flow of bait in a constant line. From the bank your loose feed is spread far and wide and so, eventually, are the fish. From a boat, feeding in a straight line is very easy. You just drop your loose feed by the anchor and it has to take the same route every time. Naturally the tackle has to be right, and in this case a three BB stick float is set a foot overdepth and held back slightly as it trots down the flow. The main line is 2.6lb breaking strain and the bait, two maggots, is impaled on a size 20 hook on a ¾lb breaking strain hook link. The swim is fed for about ten minutes in which time I set up my live-baiting rod and perhaps have a cup of coffee and a sandwich. All of the time that early morning sun is warming my back and there is not usually another pike angler in sight. Most other pike anglers, by now, have changed their snap tackles for bolt-rigs. I am out on my own and that is how I like it! I love pike fishing above all else but bait catching becomes so engrossing at times, that I have often forsaken a couple of hours' piking and kept on filling the keepnet with chub and dace.

The first cast invariably brings a bite, perhaps after trotting 30 or 40 yards downstream. Generally, it is a chub or less than twelve ounces and occasionally a small roach or a roach-bream

In blazing sunshine, this river fourteen-pounder took a trotted livebait.

hybrid. The small chub of about six or seven inches and the hand-sized hybrids are the ones I want for baits. The rest are just sheer fun to catch. The number I take depends on the length of the session to come. For an average day about twenty is right but if I should run out when the pike are 'mad-on', there are other tactics that I can use which I shall come to later. On a longer session I usually catch baits as I need them rather than keeping them for ages in a keepnet. They do not stay in good condition in a net anyway and a lively bait is essential on this river.

As each trot down with the float takes place, the bites get closer and closer, provided that I keep the maggots trickling in. Eventually the fish are feeding mid-water, almost next to the boat. The only problem now is when to stop! After acquiring the baits needed, I get into the 'just one more cast' syndrome, and have been known to carry on for hours! Sometimes the pike themselves are calling me to stop as they swirl in the current and wreak havoc amongst the prey shoals.

STUDYING THE CONTOURS

One of the things I like about boat fishing on a river is that only one rod is needed at a time. To control the boat and fish with more than one rod is not easy and I find it far more productive and less frustrating to concentrate my efforts into the one. My time is spent, not only fishing, but also studying the contours of the river which will, in time, increase my catch rate from the knowledge that I gain. It is impossible to learn about a section of river overnight. From the bank it can take quite a while but from a boat there is an obvious advantage. In years past, when fishing was far less sophisticated, it was a matter of plumbing each swim that you came to and, when trotting baits down the river, making mental notes of where all the snags were. Plumbing moving water is much easier and more accurate from a boat when you can get right above it. Nowadays it is far less complicated and modern anglers can do the job quickly and very accurately using electronic depth finders, some of which can actually print out a

permanent chart showing bottom contours and features. Finding features on the Severn certainly pays off. In time you will learn that what looks like a plain piece of water at the surface can be very deceiving. The features below a weirpool are particularly fascinating once you understand them.

In the main river there can be quite considerable depth variations from one section to another and from one side of the river to the other. Huge pieces of debris brought down by the floods can result in amazing structures emerging from the bottom, ranging from large branches to fully grown trees. As these features settle they become festooned with weed and other debris and eventually become silted over to form large obstructions. A typical winter flood consisting of an extra 15 feet of power-packed current will then wash it all away and it will settle somewhere else until, many years hence, it is claimed by the sea.

Below weirs, the vagaries of the currents form drop-offs both gentle and sudden and these are subject to change as the years roll by. Flood debris is littered everywhere and collects particularly beneath the concrete sill. All this probably sounds like an angler's nightmare but this is the key to finding the fish. I have long believed that river pike move around the river from one structure to another, using these as both resting and ambush points. Find these features and the pike are not usually far away.

The most fabulous example of such a swim was the huge tree that came over Upper Lode weir on the Severn in the late seventies and settled just below the end of the island. The lucky few pikers that were there in the early days enjoyed fabulous catches of pike to over 20lb before, it silted over several years later. Then there was the 'log-hole' swim, just upstream, with a heavy, solid obstacle embedded into the bed of the river. Some say it was connected to the large sunken tree but whether it was or was not, it was another very reliable spot to catch pike from. From the bank, the extent of features like these could only be estimated but from the boat you could get right over them and often see the ones that emerged quite close to the surface when the river ran clear.

The snag in the 'log-hole' could actually be prodded with an outstretched oar and its position and depth accurately gauged. Many a haul came from it simply by anchoring 20 yards upstream and trotting livebaits about a foot above it or working a deep diving plug over it. When working a 28g, red-head pattern Abu Hi-Lo, one had to reel quite hard to get down near it and at times the plug could be felt hitting it. As soon as this is felt, the pressure is eased off to allow it to rise over it. That is where the takes come, right next to it. In a river, the current, luckily, works in your favour to release snagged buoyant lures.

The huge sunken tree was quite a problem to fish as there was just so much under the water that snagging up was a very real probability and we did not risk the lures there. The number of pike snagged and lost by pikers in that swim was legendary but I can say, in all honesty, that it never happened to me, either from the bank or boat. Strong tackle and firm pressure are essential in these situations or all is lost.

WEIRPOOL PIKING

One of my favourite spots, for there were so many, was immediately below the sill of the weir right in amongst the churning white water. The concrete apron is shaped such that there is, for much of its length, a sharp drop off into deep water. This means that the fast torrent affects the upper layer of water only and down below the water is hardly affected at all. There are treacherous undercurrents there though, which are constantly changing with river levels. It took quite a while to pluck up the courage to try fishing this area but when I did I was pleasantly surprised, not only to find how easy it was, but also about the huge numbers of pike sheltering down there.

The first thing to do when weirpool fishing is to anchor up safely and in doing so make as little disturbance as possible. A piker with little experience could be forgiven for thinking that the task was not only dangerous but also impossible. It is

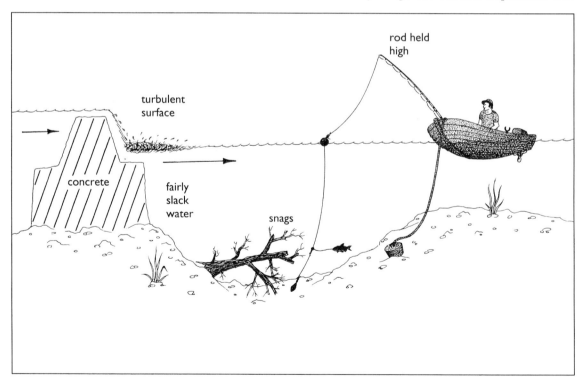

Cross-section of a typical weirpool.

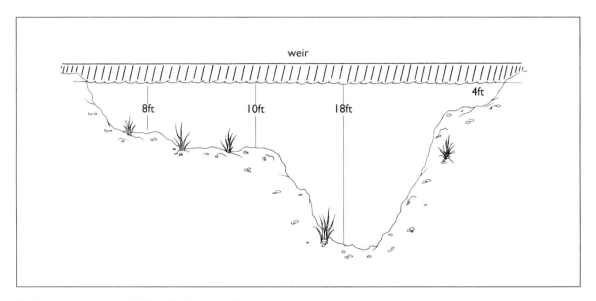

Section across a weirpool. Plumbing is essential.

very dangerous when the river reaches a certain level. It is doubly dangerous when there is a high tide due that could push your boat into the suction of the weir. I cannot stress strongly enough to anyone reading this book, that this is a very hazardous practice and unless you know exactly what you are doing, keep away from it.

The procedure that I use, although I am not recommending that anyone else be so foolhardy, is to get as close as possible to the sill and drop the anchor onto the base of the slope of the concrete apron. I let out the rope until I am in a safe position and then gently tug the anchor until it slips over the ledge and drops immediately underneath it into deep water where it takes hold. I then take up the slack rope until I am anchored in the desired position. Sometimes the boat gets washed away if the anchor does not get a good grip and you have to do it all over again. Some days, with the river carrying extra water, you have to abandon the plan altogether. It is much better to have two anglers in the boat when doing this as one can control the boat and the other one positions the anchor. At first, every part of the weir looks the same but over time I have learned that some places are far better than others due to the unseen features beneath the surface.

When in position, I usually like to let everything settle for ten minutes or so while the swim quietens down and I make sure that I am going to be safe. An upstream wind may, for example, cause the boat to keep turning into the sill and drawing it crossways into the churning water. This certainly makes the heart jump a little. A way round this is to hang the landing net over the back of the boat so that the current is constantly pulling it in a downstream direction and keeping you straight. Once you are confident, the fishing can start. I have three methods that I employ and I find it hard to say which I enjoy the most.

Lure fishing

The first method is lure fishing. Initially, it was very easy to catch on lures. This was probably a sign of naive fish. After a season or so, this method tailed off considerably in effectiveness. The lures that worked best of all were the big, slow-working plugs like the Abu 40g Hi-Lo and the Storm 'Big Mac', worked deep in the water. This caught pike of all sizes to ounces short of 20lb. Another effective plug was the large Heddon 'Prowler' but I stopped using it because it seemed to damage the pikes' teeth as it was so big and hard.

An Abu 40g Hi-Lo accounted for this 15lb river pike on a July morning.

Opposite
A mid-double from the weirpool on paternostered chub livebait.

Pike of all sizes took our big plugs.

A big problem is that big plugs mean expensive plugs and if you are going to lose them anywhere then this is the place! Usually, I had to work them deep near the snags to get a take and, every now and again, the inevitable happened. On one occasion, my fishing partner Bob 'Jacko' Jackson and I lost three expensive plugs in as many casts. Maybe that was why our catches on plugs started to dwindle – because we were too anxious to lower them right down to where the pike were feeding!

Paternostered Livebait

The best way to get right down into the pikes' lair was to paternoster a livebait. At first it seemed an impossibility to get a bait to hold under the sill but it did not take me long to find out that it could be done. I started by using a 2oz bomb on a standard

The boat allowed us to get baits right under the sill.

sunken float paternoster rig as I thought that the whole lot would be easily dragged out of position. This did not happen and so I tried a lighter weight, until eventually I found that my standard ¾oz bomb held quite easily but I had to fish in a certain manner. This involved casting the rig and bait under the sill and then holding the rod high in the air to keep the line off the water. The tackle would, generally, hold there indefinitely, though this was not often necessary.

It was a rare day that I did not catch on this rig and some huge hauls of pike came out. When the takes came, they were something to really savour. While waiting for a 'take', the bale-arm is open and the line is held on the spool with the first finger. The line is held tight, right through to the bait. As a pike takes, the feeling is transmitted right through to the rod arm in the form of a dull thud. Time and time again I have trembled with

excitement as a take has taken me by surprise. As with all my baits, I am rigged for striking within a few seconds of the take and the first few seconds of the fight are critical. It is important to be absolutely sure that you know what to do when you hook a power-packed predator in such a dangerous situation.

It is not advisable to stand up. I prefer to kneel down on the padding in the bottom of the boat. Tighten up to the pike, keep the pressure on and be sure you know which side of the anchor rope it has gone. Guide him down stream away from the snaggy sill area with the objective of fighting him from the back of the boat. If you do this wrongly you can be in a lot of trouble. Unexpected things can and do happen and here are just two of them. The pike might head across and under the sill, turning the boat crossways on to the current and putting you in a precarious position especially if there is a strong upstream wind blowing. On another occasion, the fight may cause the anchor to lose its grip and you could end up drifting down into deeper water with the anchor off bottom. In very little time, you could be drifting downstream through a bank angler's swim and getting ensnared in willow branches. There are no hard and fast rules about what to do in these circumstances. Should you start drifting, ensure that you have made a quick-release knot in the anchor rope that can be released with one hand. Do so and let the rope out to its fullest extent, about twice the maximum depth of the water is best, and you should come to a safe halt. Know your equipment and your own capabilities and you will get out of trouble somehow!

Wobbled Deadbait

The third tactic to mention for tackling weirpool pike is the wobbled deadbait. This is a deadly method anywhere and yet one sadly neglected by most pike anglers. On a river where you might be constantly on the move and using searching tactics, no method could be more suitable. The rig is exactly as that described in Chapter Two for still waters and can be used equally effectively in moving water. It scores particularly well in moving water as the current imparts more life to it and the faster the water, the slower the retrieve that can be achieved. That is not to say that a slow retrieve is always important. Sometimes, river pike will go for a bait that is very rapidly wound back and many times I have had pike grab in this way when all I intended to do was to get the bait back quickly either to check it or move to another swim. Varying the speed of retrieve is as important as retrieving at the correct depth. On the weirpools, any fish bait is suitable for wobbling but small chub have a big advantage in that they cast like bullets. Sea baits are usually a poor second choice but will do if nothing else is available.

Varying the style of retrieve is often a good idea but I have no firm views on river pike showing a preference during summer conditions. I have had as many pike on steady retrieves as on jerky, sink-and-draw types and use both styles until something takes it. If possible I like to allow my bait to sink right to the bottom and leave it there for a while but a lot of tackle can be lost in weirpools if you are not familiar with the swims. If you use this technique, make the bait buoyant by injecting it with air from a syringe and add sufficient swan shots to the trace to make it sink to the bottom but with the bait standing proud of it. This certainly reduces the number of times that you snag up badly on general weirpool debris, but, of course, if there is a sunken tree in the swim, nothing will help matters!

Making baits buoyant with polystyrene or balsa sticks is not a good idea where there is a good chance you will lose them. They might eventually get picked up by a pike. Pike do pick up these snagged baits and I have seen them caught with baited traces inside them from baits snagged and lost earlier in the day.

As with lure fishing, the takes on the wobbled deadbaits vary quite considerably, and anything from a slight knock to an arm-stopping wrench can be expected. When to strike is not a problem if you are using sensibly sized baits. Small baits up to four inches long can be struck immediately as one would when lure fishing. Bigger baits from four to six inches need a few seconds longer. Having watched many pike grab such baits in clear water, I have noticed that they either have the hooks in their mouth anyway or sometimes gently let go and make a lightning second grab which sees the bait turned and then passed further into its jaws. A five-second wait with a bait of this size usually sees a successful hooking.

With larger baits, you will experience one of two things. You may wait a sensible time, say ten seconds, and then strike. As a result, you will find that several fish drop off through not being properly hooked and you will never know just how big they were. Alternatively, you may be totally irresponsible, with no one there to see you, and leave the bait too long. A good proportion will be landed without dropping off but many will be deep hooked! Sensibly sized baits catch me plenty of pike including many big ones. I use them all the time now and avoid the problems and heartaches of losing pike that come off.

Whichever method you use for tackling weirpool pike from a boat, in time you will catch some, but special care needs to be taken when returning these fish. On a still water it is easy to watch a pike swim safely away but on a churning river pool it is not so obvious that this has happened. Do not just drop pike back over the side into the turbulent water. If one should be distressed it could quite easily be swept away with the current and you would never know about it. The best thing to do is to hold them in the landing net at the back of the boat in the patch of calm water that is created and only release them when they are raring to go.

Weirpool piking is dangerous. Some weirs are extremely dangerous places to be, especially in unpredictable water conditions and bad weather. It is hard work too but this should not stop you from tackling these places if you want to taste the action. As long as you realize your limitations and do not go too far, there is no reason at all why you should not take part.

Weir piking can be a marvellous summer activity but of course, not every one is lucky enough to live within striking distance of such a weir. The quality of the pike fishing that I have experienced at such places, although not unique, is quite rare during this hot, sticky month. In the cool, well-oxygenated waters of a weirpool, there are bound to be concentrations of fish of all species which must improve one's chances considerably.

On other waters, however, bear in mind that all pike have to eat and when the water is warm, as in this month, the rate at which the pike uses up its energy is high and it needs a much larger food intake that it would in the colder months. As this is the case, one might well ask why pike fishing is not at its best in the summer on all other waters. The simple answer appears to me to be that although the pike hunts much more actively

In a world of my own.

when water temperatures are higher, the fact that prey fish are often more openly abundant means that it can satisfy itself very, very quickly. It may take all it needs for a day in a quick foray at dawn or whenever it chooses to make its move.

NOCTURNAL PIKE

My experience when fishing for other species during this month has shown that pike can be active at all times of the day and night. Possibly they feed, at times, at a leisurely browsing pace because they know that there is such an abundance of food about. Consequently, they seem to take baits at all sorts of odd times. The extent of night feeding by pike interests me, especially in the summer, and it may have been underestimated in the past.

I have very firm views on nocturnal pike fishing. Although night fishing for pike in summer is a very good way of catching them, I will not do it! Night fishing during July, for eels and zander, has always been a favourite pastime of mine and naturally, by using fish baits I am likely to attract the odd pike. In actual fact, I have caught so many pike on small fish baits and pieces of fish, that I know that summer night fishing for pike would be a very productive exercise. Many a 'record zander' or 'monster eel' has suddenly turned into a good pike as it has rolled over my landing net in the torch light! Virtually every pike caught accidently at night has been deep hooked. The vigilance required to prevent this is beyond the capabilities of most anglers. With the best intentions in the world and first class bite indication systems most anglers cannot strike runs at night in sufficient time to prevent this from happening! I have walked past bivvys with alarms screaming and anglers snoring away inside! I have even landed other anglers' fish, rebaited and recast for them, while they have slept on! Summer nights can be extremely cold so all but the bravest get comfortably wrapped in blankets or a sleeping bag and they inevitably nod off! Pike wolf baits down very quickly when the water temperature is high and you have only a few seconds to respond. Most times you just cannot do it properly at night and deep hooking will be the result.

Removing Deep-Seated Hooks

If the hooks are barbless or semi-barbless, their removal can be effected fairly easily in most instances. If the hooks are barbed, their removal can severely damage pike! The technique is not easy in the daylight and for an inexperienced angler to attempt it in the dark would be disastrous. The technique involves pulling on the trace with a measured degree of pressure until the shank of the first treble is exposed. The forceps are inserted through the gill opening and the hook is turned to release it from the flesh. Further gentle pressure is then applied until the second treble is exposed. By this time a good deal of the pike's stomach will be in its throat!

The second hook is turned and released. If the hooks are barbed, a lot of tearing will take place! The stomach must then be gently eased back into position. To attempt this in the pitch black with a thrashing pike would be a nightmare leading to serious damage to the pike. Very often, pulling at the trace will not move the hooks as they have pierced the stomach wall and caught up either in vital organs or the body cavity lining. That pike will probably die! I have unhooked many pike hooked in this way by inexperienced pike anglers and know that it is very damaging. A solitary angler using such poor practice could wipe out a good pike water in a very short time. Should you wish to night fish for pike in a responsible manner, a good idea is to purchase a headband-mounted torch to ensure that both hands are free, making the unhooking task so much easier.

As if the damage caused by hooks was not a good enough reason for not night fishing for summer pike, there is another problem that will make things even worse. Many waters will be heavily weeded at this time of the season and clear pits and the shallow end of reservoirs will be particularly affected. Hooked pike will have to be hauled through it. Even in the daylight this can be a difficult task and the pike themselves do not help matters by fighting like the clappers and boring into it. Indeed, on some pits, I will not even attempt to catch pike from them until late October simply because I do not have a reasonable chance of landing them, due to snagging up. Fish that are deep-hooked and then lost and possibly tethered in weed on a broken line will be very likely to die. Remember that! I have painted a very black picture of night piking in the summer because I believe that it could lead to waters being ruined through loss of fish. With correct choice of water and extreme vigilance it can be done properly but I would suggest that it requires a very special angler to be able to do so.

Other Nocturnal Predators

So what of my own predator fishing in the dark in summer? The same rules still apply of course to eels, perch and zander. These species are just as likely to suffer a similar fate as the pike if proper procedures are not adhered to. I rarely night fish for pike and perch because I can catch them in the daytime in sufficient numbers not to feel that I have to do so. Eels and zander are different and there are times when night fishing is the only way to catch them. This being the case, I stick to a procedure that keeps deep hooking to a bare minimum. The basic rules that I use could equally well apply to pike.

I do not sleep. The best way to ensure that is to sit on an ordinary chair and not a bed chair. I sit close to the rods and am aware of the start to each run. Most importantly of all, I use a method that gives immediate indication of a run. Free-lining is completely out as this method has probably accounted for more deep-hooked predators than any other because the fish can move a long way before a run is registered at the rod. A few anglers are very good at setting up their tackle in such a way that runs from free-lining can be detected quite quickly, but most anglers are not!

Some sunken float paternoster rigs are equally inefficient, namely the type where the fish drags the whole rig along. The rigs where the paternoster link stays still and the main line is pulled through it are much better and this is the type that I prefer for fishing eel and zander baits off bottom. The rig that I use can fish baits right up to the surface and I am often amazed that pike, well into double figures, bother to take small fish sections like this. Bottom baits are fished on standard leger rigs which show any runs almost immediately. Having a rig that shows a run straight away is only useful if you have the will to strike quickly. If you are regularly deep-hooking fish you must look at your tackle and your attitude and do something about it. It is no good blaming the fish, as many do, for wolfing the baits down when you, yourself, are creating the problem.

MINI-PIKING

Everything seems better in the light of day and nothing more so than piking. To me, it is not just catching pike that counts but enjoying it too. There can be a big difference between the two if you stop and think about it. The most intriguing and interesting piking that I have ever done has been for pike weighing less than one pound in weight! I suppose you could call it mini-piking! I love summer fishing on the gin clear gravel pits for all species and in particular perch. While fishing for them with fish baits, pike naturally figure in the catches. I have forsaken fishing for big cruising carp just to indulge in a fascinating hour or two with them on my favourite waters in July. If you keep the maggots flowing into the marginal reeded swims, you will soon attract hordes of fry. These in turn attract perch.

Most perch are small, under half a pound but holding back you can see the shadows of much bigger ones. I have two rods set up. One is for catching the tiddlers on maggots, and the other is set up for the perch. This is really standard tench float tackle with a size 10 or 12 hook, tied directly to 6lb line. A small fish of about two inches is caught and then transferred, alive or dead, to the hook of the tench tackle and cast back into the swim. The float is undershotted so that about an inch is showing and the depth is set to around mid-water. As it drifts round, and if the perch want it, away it sails. The takes are fantastic and the perch pull the float a foot or more under the surface. In amongst them, naturally, come the pike.

From an early age pike feed on small fish as well as anything else that moves, such as beetles, larvae and shrimps. Even the smallest ones cannot resist a tiny roach in distress and I have been fascinated to catch them as little as three inches long with the roach wedged into their tiny snouts. Sometimes when playing a small pike, a slightly bigger one grabs it or a big perch chases it. The numbers of these smaller pike, the ones that you would normally not catch, can be phenomenal and at times whole armies of them are seen to come in to attack the bait. Most of these will be eaten by big pike during the summer in the normal course of events but if a couple of big pike are either killed or removed, there is the possibility of a temporary situation where small pike are numerous.

OPPORTUNIST PIKING

Sometimes, when enjoying my other summer fishing, I don't set out to catch pike but the temptation can be too much when they appear in my swim. On local pits and drains, I often clear holes in the weed for roach and tench fishing. These holes, surrounded by weed, make excellent ambush points for pike and sometimes they drive me crazy when I want to get on with some other fishing. The holes are baited with hemp, tares and corn and before long, roach and tench move in. In some swims I can see the bottom and actually watch the fish. Just as I am getting down to catching a few, very often a good take from an unseen force makes me think that I have got a really good tench on. Then it lets go and a jaw-marked roach comes flapping to the surface. Where I know this happens regularly, I have a pike rod ready made up for paternostering a small livebait. When pike are in this mood, nothing else will do. They do not want a deadbait and it is difficult to present a lure or wobbled bait into the weed where they are hiding in ambush. They are waiting down there for one of those roach to step out of line.

The head of a large pike.

Sometimes the pike do not give themselves away by grabbing fish. Their very presence, however, is enough to stop the roach from feeding and a sudden halt to the sport usually means that one or more has moved in. It could lie there for hours so you might just as well catch it! Unfortunately the sport is wrecked for a while afterwards so all you can do is rebait the swim and leave it while you stretch your legs and have a cup of tea. Carry the pike a few swims away, put it gently into a weedbed and hope it stays there! Sometimes it gets quite hectic and I catch as many pike as I would on some autumn and winter days. Fun fishing at its best!

If you do decide to fish for pike in July whether in a well organized or casual way, it is important to treat them with more than the normal care and respect that they deserve. You will certainly not be disappointed if you are looking for a hard powerful fight and they will often jump clear of the water in the process. This, of course, is tiring them out badly and the last thing they need then is to go through a lengthy unhooking operation. Neither should they want to be retained in sacks and nets for any length of time. Pike caught in summer will flap about on the bank far more than winter pike will, so find somewhere soft to place them and firmly, but gently, restrain them from harming themselves. If possible put them straight back, if necessary, allowing them to lie quietly in the margin until they are ready to go. Keep an eye on them for a while to make sure that they have recovered. If you must take photographs at least make sure that you have planned ahead how you will do it. If you are with a friend, it can be all over in seconds but if alone, just hold the fish in the landing net supported on sticks or rod-rests to keep it upright, while you set up the camera and tripod. One shot of a nice, clean, healthy looking pike is worth a hundred shots of a tatty one that has been mistreated.

Returning a livebait-caught eighteen pounder to the River Severn.

5 AUGUST – LURED AWAY

August is the frustrating month. It is hardly a month that one associates with pike fishing yet it has given me some remarkably enjoyable piking days. It has never been a month to provide me with huge hauls or particularly big fish but it has given me a lot of pleasure and that is what matters. By picking and choosing times, places and tactics, the keen pike angler can carry on with his pleasure even at this most unlikely time of year.

Summer reaches its height in August and, in many places, so does the dreaded weed. This is the pike angler's curse now, but later in the year we will be thankful for it. When the weed starts to die back, find the remaining areas of cover and you will be sure that the pike are not too far away. For now, you can either let it beat you and fish for something else or find ways of catching pike despite this annoying problem. On many waters, in particular where the water is very clear, weed is often excessive as a result, not only of nature, but also of man's over-enrichment of the environment as a result of excessive use of agricultural fertilizers. With such widespread cover, the pike can be found virtually anywhere, moving silently and craftily from one patch of weed to another. Indeed, some waters become one massive weed bed and the pike can cover the whole place, unseen by man or prey. Whether pike actually travel beneath the weed when hunting is debatable. I tend to think that generally they do not as they are so well camouflaged that they are barely discernible anyway as they pass quietly over the weed. Remember too that the pike's prey will, during the warmer months, be up in the higher water layers and may not see the pike creeping up so easily. The pike's eyes are in an ideal position for keeping a lookout above him when he is in an alert mode.

In deep water, even where there is no weed, the pike may decide to take its stance at any depth and this is important to bear in mind. This in particular is a time of year when it is possible to make the mistake of fishing a bait too deep, I have taken many pike, both large and small, by drifting and trolling livebaits and working lures and wobbled baits just a couple of feet beneath the surface, over much deeper water. Similar deep fished baits have been less effective as they are either ignored or – and this is more likely – unnoticed by pike. Pike in these gin-clear, weedy, waters are amongst the most beautiful that you are likely to encounter, being very vividly marked in dark shades of green and silvery yellow. We all like the fun of catching the pike but there is more to it than that for the discerning piker. Simply to gaze upon such pike for a few seconds before we slip them back is, to many of us, a joy in itself. They do not have to be twenty-pounders either for even the smallest of pike can give pleasure in this way.

So, with pike moving around under cover of weed and likely to be found anywhere, for me this means using an effective searching technique, at least until I have worked out where they are on a particular water. Cover a lot of water and you must increase your chances of covering and, it is hoped, tempting more fish. Remember too, that the pike we are seeking will not always be feeding or even alert at all times throughout the long summer days.

I have already mentioned drifting and trolling livebaits. On the bigger, deeper waters these can be most effective fish-finding techniques but unfortunately, it is not so easy to find places in England today where one can widely practise these methods, especially in summer when other waters users are active. The alternative, and one being employed more and more by many anglers, is lure fishing. It is not a technique relegated to high summer of course but as I tend to employ this technique a lot at this time, this is as good a place as any to look at what is involved for those with limited experience. The modern piker would be unwise to ignore lure fishing for, in time, should livebaiting become outlawed widely it will be a vital weapon in the piker's armoury when the pike want a moving target. It is not a skill that can be learned overnight either, despite its being a method often associated with novices and casual anglers.

I am always staggered when I hear quite experienced pike men say that lure fishing is not their scene and that they cannot get on with it. I cannot understand this attitude. Imagine that you are slowly working a sub-surface lure across a slightly rippled gravel pit on a warm August morning. Your attention is wandering slightly as you take in the beauty of it all, when suddenly everything stops dead for an instant and you cannot wind in any further. The water heaves as your arm muscles tense. Something has taken that lure with an awesome finality and you sweep the rod back. Before you have reached the vertical the rod lunges back down and three feet of green and yellow clears the water as the clutch screams. That is piking at its best and anyone who says they cannot get into it must be doing something dreadfully wrong or is fishing for the wrong reasons. Good pike fishing is not just about catching the biggest fish. Remember also that lure fishing is only one part of the wonderful world of piking and you do not have to miss out on the other methods. If you fish the best tactics for the prevailing conditions, you can do it all.

Before going further in describing tackle and tactics for the lure angler, may I point out something else. I prefer to lure fish in mid-summer but that is not to say that there are not other approaches that will work on occasions. Apart from those already mentioned, other tactics normally associated with colder conditions, like static deadbaiting, can work too. It is a matter of being in the right place at the right time. When

the pike are really going for it, particularly for a very brief spell at daybreak, deadbaits will be effective if you can find out where the pike are feeding. This has been the case on several drains and reservoirs where I have summer fished. Some waters become the exception to the rule and make very viable mid-summer pike waters where you can catch at almost any time of the day. I am thinking here of my experience on the River Severn weirpools where I enjoyed sport with pike in the midday August sun for many a season. If you really want pike fishing badly enough, if you search far and wide enough you will find some whatever the time of year. Effort is the key word!

As I live now in an area rich in pike waters, my lure rod is permanently made up in the garage. My current circumstances often find that I only have a couple of hours to fish at a time. It would hardly be worth the trouble of sorting out all the gear for multi-rod bait fishing for such a short session. The minimal tackle required for lure fishing is so simple that I can be away within five minutes of deciding to go. In actual fact, I find lure fishing to be more enjoyable on these regular short sessions. Perhaps it is because I know that I can always go back tomorrow if I want to, that I feel that two or three hours is enough. Done properly, lure fishing can be quite tiring. It involves casting every minute or so, being continually on your feet, climbing up and down banks and getting into awkward places to give them a try. Compare this to bait fishing where it is possible to cast out and then relax for a couple of hours.

Lure fishing is definitely the best way to go about piking if your time is severely rationed. If you can make those valuable hours coincide with feeding times so much the better but remember that a well-presented lure might just tempt an immobile pike to snap at it when it might choose to ignore a nearby deadbait. Also bear in mind that many more pike will see a lure than a static fish bait. My short lure fishing sessions in recent summers have produced pike to 28lb 12oz but I would have been just as happy with the fun that I have had from the hundreds of smaller pike caught. For me at least, I suppose, 'fun' is the word that sums lure fishing up.

LURE RODS

What makes the ideal rod for lure fishing is one of those subjects that has received no end of debate and my conclusion is that you should use something that you are happy with. Rod length, for example, is very variable. Rods from as short as 6 feet to as long as 12 feet are employed. Why such a variation? Many of the top lure anglers employ short rods, often in conjunction with small multiplying reels. These lightweight outfits are particularly ideal for boat anglers especially if they are fishing non-stop for eight, ten or twelve hours a day or even longer. Correctly designed rods will handle any pike you are likely to encounter even if they appear flimsy.

At the other extreme, some anglers are using light carp rods of 11 to 12 feet in length in conjunction with fixed spool reels. So why do serious anglers, in some instances, choose to fish in this way? If you are regularly fishing reed and tree-lined banks, a long rod is essential for casting round corners in this terrain and, most importantly, to guide fish around these bankside obstacles when playing them. You can also use this set-up from a boat if this is something that you will only do once in a while, but you may in the long term find it cumbersome and heavy. The same versatility would not be possible with the short rod set-up, as, on the awkward banks described, they may be impossible to use. If you are really serious about lure fishing you will probably end up with several sets of tackle which will allow you to use the best one for the situation in hand.

The tackle that I use for most of my lure fishing today is what I would call a mid-range set-up. It will flick out quite small spinners and yet still throw 40g spoons to the horizon. It comprises an 11-foot, 1lb 10oz test curve through-action carbon fibre rod built for me by Bruce and Walker and now marketed as the MB 4 Waterwolf. It is very light and slim but at the same time it has quite thick walls and the mechanical strength to withstand being bashed around in boats and in the back of the car. Modern materials ensure that despite the thickness of the wall on this blank, it is still very light and not a problem to fish with all day long. There are many similar blanks available today, usually sold as carp rods and at prices to suit all pockets. The one that I use is fitted with eight silicone carbide rings plus tip ring. These rings are very expensive although not essential as there are many other excellent lined rings around. However, silicone carbide with its much reduced friction properties gives a much smoother feel when casting and playing hooked fish. In lure fishing, where a lot of casting is done and usually more fish are caught than on other rods, this to me seems to be an ideal application. In conclusion, I recommend that you give deep thought to where and how your lure fishing is to be carried out and choose a rod to suit.

LURE REELS

Reels for lure fishing also provide endless debate. I have always been perfectly happy with a small fixed spool reel and have fished alongside many others using multipliers. I can fish just as happily and effectively using my reel as they do with theirs. They will argue that they can cast just as far as I can. This is rarely the case, especially with very light lures. They will tell me that they are more in control when playing a lively fish. I would not argue with that, but I don't find myself with any worries on that score anyway. Certainly rods with multipliers stow away nicely in the boat compared to fixed spool reels that can get in the way but at the end of the day it is up to the individual to decide what is best for him. It takes time to become proficient with a multiplier and enjoy the small benefits that they offer. Many just use them because they have the right image. I just wryly smile as I carry on fishing while they spend another quarter of an hour sorting out the plague of the multiplier reel – the over-run! The principle of using the thumb to slow down the reel spool at the end of the cast is, in theory, quite sound. In practice, I have seen even the best pikers make a hash of it and get the line in an enormous tangle!

In my opinion, multipliers are of little benefit to the general lure angler especially in view of the great improvements in modern fixed spool reels, notably better designed spools to give longer, smoother casting and also more efficient clutches that avoid the jerkiness which might bounce a lure from a pike's jaw. However, should you decide to specialize in lure fishing, you will, in time, reap the benefits offered by the multiplier as you become proficient with one. The occasional user will find them very frustrating to use. These are the facts; the choice is yours.

LINE FOR LURE FISHING

The choice of line for lure fishing is important. Lure fishing naturally entails a lot of casting and retrieving which results in a lot of wear and tear on line. Lines need to come off the spool cleanly without coiling and should also have very good abrasion-resistance qualities. They need good wet-knot strength too, due to the regular violent snatches made by pike at the rod tip. The line must also be fairly inconspicuous in the water. Fortunately, many modern lines meet this criteria. The lines that I recommend are exactly the same as those that I recommend for my general fishing for big pike, namely Berkeley Big Game and Bagley's Silver Thread AN 40.

I feel reluctant to recommend any line of less that 12lb breaking strain to beginners. However, there is a case for using lighter lines in certain circumstances. This might be, for example, to work lures slowly in shallow clear water or to lend a more tempting action to certain types of lures. These are lessons that I learned from continental anglers who lure fish all the time. Even they, expert as they may be, admit to being broken occasionally on light tackle. I cannot accept this risk in my fishing and continue to use 12lb breaking strain even if it reduces the number of fish I catch. Using an even heavier breaking strain makes lure fishing very difficult but in extremely snaggy swims this may be necessary.

LANDING LURE-CAUGHT PIKE

Having chosen rods, reels and lines to suit your lure fishing, you may be surprised to find that choosing the rest of the tackle, notably the lures themselves, is even more complicated. The lure angler seems to carry so little tackle with him. That is one of the benefits of lure fishing of course. However, those few items have to be very carefully chosen in order to keep the bulk down as lure fishing is all about mobility. All lure anglers should take a landing net with them, but it is surprising just how many you see without one, the reason usually being that they are only expecting to catch small pike. Some of these men are a real danger to our sport and need educating if we are going to stop them from doing any more damage. They can usually land the jacks by hand, as anyone can, but when a bigger fish comes along they may decide to beach it without considering that the bank may be rough and the fish will flap all over the place. I have even seen these types put their foot on the fish to hold it steady. Worse still, there are a few fishermen who still use a gaff but, thankfully, they are a dying breed.

The serious pike angler will always take a net with him. However, sometimes the worst thing that you can do is net a lure-caught pike. The possibility of hooks snagging in the mesh presents the lure angler with a very serious dilemma. Small fish up to 7 or 8lb are not too difficult for most of us to land by hand, but above this they get more troublesome especially in the warmer months when they are very lively or when the bankside terrain is awkward, so the landing net would appear to be the only option. If you are using a simple lure like a spoon with a solitary treble, there should not be any problems. The chances are that the hook will be almost wholly inside the pike's mouth and will not create a tricky situation.

However, imagine the worst scenario. You have hooked a very big lively pike on a large plug that has three large trebles and two of them are outside the pike's mouth. You may feel that you cannot land that fish by hand or would find it impossible to do so due to the nature of the bank, so you decide to net it. The first danger is that the flying trebles will catch on the net before the pike has gone in. It might twist and wriggle until it breaks free and in doing so, could tear its mouth. That is probably preferable to what might happen otherwise. If the fish started thrashing and spinning round, as they often do, the net and pike could get in a terrible tangle which might damage both fish and net in the frantic, long-winded struggle. This can and certainly does happen if you are not experienced. If the truth is to be told, it can also happen, now and again, even if you are!

Minimizing Problems

The problems caused by netting can be reduced, to some extent, by reducing the number of hooks on lures. Many of my plugs that originally had two trebles now only have one and those that had three now have two. My recent twenty-eight-pounder came on a sinking plug on which I had reduced the number of trebles from three to two. Both hooks were caught outside the jaw and because I had modified the trebles in this way minimized the potential risk of tangling. One might think that using barbless or semi-barbless hooks would be a sensible idea too but those who have tried it, myself included, have concluded that this is not advisable because too many fish drop off and are lost.

It is also sensible to reduce the size of hooks to something you feel is adequate for giving a reliable hookhold. Many lures are designed as sea lures and are sold with heavy-gauge, corrosion-resistant hooks. These can be replaced with something more delicate. They will still snag but with thinner wire and smaller barbs should be much easier to remove. They are much kinder to the pike's jaws too!

Most popular large nets have quite small mesh and consequently trebles of all types get very badly ensnared in them. There are a few nets around now that have a soft, sack-like bottom section and quite large mesh above this. They are actually intended for carp and allow easier passage of the net through the water when netting a big fish. When the fish is lifted, the soft sacking in the bottom will not rub and damage it. I find

Modified lures: top, replace large thick wire hooks with smaller, less damaging ones: bottom, remove unnecessary hooks to reduce unhooking problems.

this type of net much more suitable for lure fishing. I use a 42-inch net, because I feel it gives me a lot of latitude in preventing a lure from catching on the mesh as I guide a fish into it. Other anglers may feel that this is too big and heavy and would forsake this benefit for the ease of carrying offered by a 36-inch net. When my 'twenty-eight' wallowed over the drawstring, I was glad of every inch! Skill and expertise can, of course, make up for net size and as huge pike on lures are the exception, a smaller, lighter net is perhaps the best general choice (Llandegfedd excepted!) With lure fishing increasing in popularity, I am sure we will soon see plenty of purpose-designed nets on the market.

LURE BOXES

What else does the lure angler carry with him? It is popular to carry the lures in a plastic tackle box. Hinged boxes of various types have, for many years, been popular with lure anglers. Lures tend to get into terrible tangles even when one starts out with the best of intentions and a box of this type, with lots of compartments, is ideal for keeping them in order. The sizes and styles of these boxes vary enormously and the latest types include easy-access side drawers. The traditional hinged box can be difficult to open at times (in a small boat, for example) and the modern side drawer types reduce this difficulty.

It can be difficult for the lure angler to decide how many lures to take with him as he can easily build up a collection of many hundreds. For short sessions, I might only take half-a-dozen tried and tested patterns. I might even carry these in my pockets with the hooks covered with plastic protectors. For a longer session, this might be a short sighted practice as there are situations where a wide variety of options need to be explored and where many different lures are used before fish are caught.

THE LURE TREE

I used to become very frustrated trying to keep my lures in some semblance of order. I was so tired of rummaging through boxes of tangled lures that I came up with the idea of a 'Lure tree'. All it consists of is three large polystyrene boxes stacked on top of each other. It sits on the work top in my tackle room and takes up only about 1½ square feet of surface area. Around the 'tree's' outer surface I can simply impale hundreds of lures. Being light and offering very little friction,

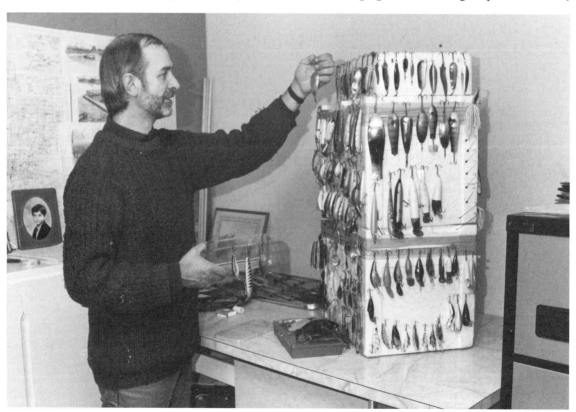

Selecting lures for a session from my 'lure tree'.

it rotates easily in order to allow lures to be examined on all faces. The lures are roughly segregated into different types: spinners, spinnerbaits, spoons, surface and shallow diving plugs, and deep diving plugs. Other types of lures such as rubber wobblers and jigs are laid out on trays so that I can see at a glance exactly what I have. I much prefer to store them in this way and select them as I need them.

Choosing lures for a fishing session is now very easy. For a short session I pack them into a small box and have a much bigger box for a longer trip. Both boxes fit into my rucksack which I like to take with me to carry weighing equipment, camera, food and drink. When I get back home I re-hang the lures on the 'tree' and they dry much better than when left in a box or out in the garage. When I am boat fishing, it is to easier to have a greater selection of lures at hand because the weight of the box is carried by the boat. On these occasions I will have my big box with me and access to lures that I would like to experiment with as well as tried-and-trusted patterns.

UNHOOKING TOOLS

Apart from the lures, there are a few items that I always carry that are specific to lure fishing. The most important are the unhooking tools. A small pair of forceps, although satisfactory generally, is not sufficient to deal with all the unhooking problems that may be encountered. Many pairs of forceps are too flimsy for gripping and teasing out large lure hooks. They need to be strong. One way of getting them to grip well is to cut them down so that only about half an inch is left beyond the pivot point. It is better still to do the job properly and use a pair of rubber-handled, long-nosed pliers. These will get hooks out much

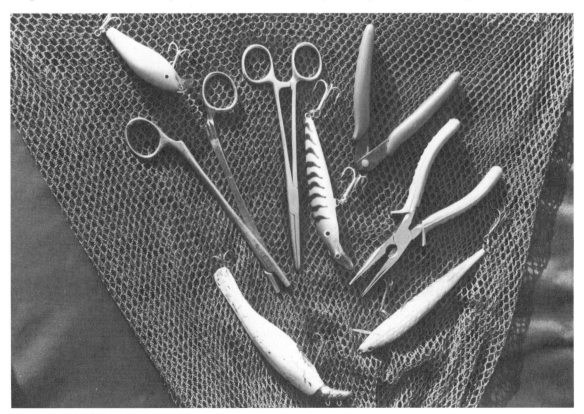

Unhooking tools for lure fishing. Fom left to right: modified forceps for stronger grip; standard forceps; wire cutters; long-nosed pliers.

more easily. However, always take your forceps for hooks that might be well inside the mouth or that might need a delicate approach through the gill cover. Carrying two pairs of forceps is often a good idea for removing multi-hook plugs. One pair is attached to a flying treble and left dangling from the jaw while a second pair (or pair of pliers) works on a more difficult hookhold inside. This stops the flying treble becoming caught up again, in the gills for example, when the pike struggles. With a deeply hooked pike, another good ploy is to cover as many flying trebles as possible with hook protectors for the same reason, while the problem hooks are worked on.

Another useful tool, though one that I hope never to have to use, is pair of wire cutters. Should the unhooking situation become dire, as it can to an inexperienced angler, the best thing to do is to cut the hooks or the offending part of the lure. This should be a rare event but bear in mind that it could arise. Although I love lure fishing I sincerely believe that this method of catching pike damages more fish than any other. However, using correct techniques can greatly reduce any possibility of this.

WIRE TRACES

The lure angler needs to carry traces to which the lures can be attached. He should always use a wire trace. It is unwise to risk not doing so even when lure fishing for perch or chub. I have taken many quality chub and perch on wire traces, enough to make me realize that to do so does not make them uncatchable.

The length of trace is often a matter of debate. A longer trace must to some extent make correct working of some lures more difficult, but it is necessary. Large spoons worked at steady retrieves often see pike hooked well at the front of the mouth and in this instance a six-inch long trace might be suitable. Small lures worked slowly near or at the surface can be hit with such force that the lure is engulfed and a 12-inch trace would not be too long. However, there is more to consider than how far the lure enters the pike's mouth. Lively pike often twist and turn and as a result the trace winds round and round the snout and catches on the lure. The line can end up actually being caught in the pike's teeth on a short trace. I may sacrifice catching a few pike

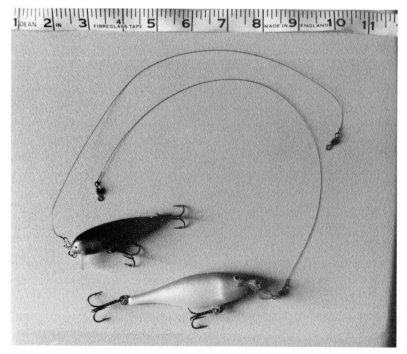

Lure traces. Note that the top trace has the wire tied direct to the snap-link to give a more delicate surface presentation.

through impairing my lure presentation but I always use a trace which is at least 12 inches long.

The breaking strain of the wire depends upon where I am fishing. Mostly it is the standard 20lb breaking strain Berkeley wire that I am happy with for most of my pike fishing. For snaggy waters, I will use the 30lb breaking strain. I am not happy with presenting lures on such heavy wire but I want to land them and not lose them!

Traces are so simple to make up having a standard Berkeley 50lb breaking strain swivel at one end and a Berkeley cross-lok swivel at the other end for attaching the lure. There are many other snap swivels on the market. Some are just as good but others have proved to be very unreliable and can spring open when under pressure. Be very careful when choosing this vital link in your tackle.

BITS AND PIECES

In the bottom of my box are lots of bits and pieces that only come out now and again for specific purposes. There is a file and a fine oilstone for sharpening hooks. When working in rocky terrain and in gravel pits, the points of trebles often need touching up. Even hooks on new lures sometimes need some attention, particularly those meant originally for sea fishing and those with large single hooks.

I also carry emery cloth and wet and dry paper. Copper and brass spoons soon become tarnished and lose their 'flash'. Sometimes this is not a bad thing and a slightly tarnished lure can often be a better catcher than a very bright new one. Should I wish to brighten one up to suit the mood of the fish, the option is there to do so.

Some lures have their hooks and lips retained with screw fittings and it is a good idea to carry a small screwdriver in case one needs replacing. Incidentally, it is also a good idea to carry a good selection of replacement hooks as they do get damaged occasionally either on snags or when unhooking fish. Additional hooks are also carried to be used as trailing trebles for situations where the pike are 'coming short'. They can be felt bumping the lure but are not being hooked.

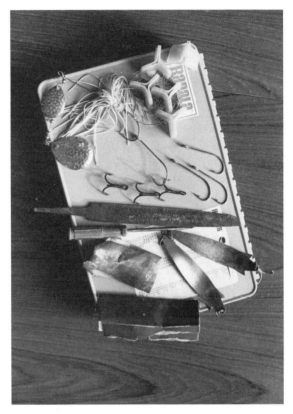

Useful items for the lure-angler to carry. Plastic hook protectors, stinger hooks, spare hooks, file, small screwdriver and fine-grade emery cloth.

Hooks, commonly known as 'stingers', can be connected on short lengths of wire or hooked directly over an existing hook and retained with a piece of rubber tubing. Purpose-made hooks with rubber moulded over the eye are also available and much easier to use.

A look through some of the American and Scandinavian lure companies' catalogues will introduce you to a whole new world of fish catching artificials and associated products. At first glance, they are completely alien to the way that we fish in the UK, but offer immense interest for those wishing to delve deeper into the world of artificial baits for catching predatory fish. My good friend, Andy Lush, at Friendly Fisherman of Tunbridge Wells, will advise you about these and any other matters concerning all the latest lure fishing products.

CHOOSING LURES

So far I have hardly mentioned the lures themselves. The subject can be so involved that confusion is bound to enter the beginner's mind. Rather than go out and buy dozens of lures, I suggest that you acquire and understand basic equipment first and be full prepared for handling pike in all sorts of difficult situations. Then you are ready to buy your first lures and begin searching the water with confidence. The actual lures that you will start with will depend upon the type of water that you will be fishing, the time of year and the condition of the water. Lures are designed to work at different depths and speeds. They have different colours and actions. They can vary enormously in size and they can give off

Different types of lures: top row, spoons; second row, spinners; third row, spinnerbaits; fourth row, surface plugs; fifth row, shallow-diving plugs; sixth row, medium depth diving plugs; bottom row, deep-diving plugs.

different visual and audible signals. Choosing the correct one is therefore not straight forward as the possible permutations are endless.

Only experience will tell you which lure to use and how to work it. Two lure anglers could look at the same situation and tackle it quite differently depending upon their previous successes on similar waters. One lure angler, when tackling a very clear pit in the late summer, might decide to start with a small, fat-bodied plug with a bold action and a rattle feature. He might work it slowly but steadily, three feet beneath the surface. Every ten seconds or so, he might slow the retrieve right down and let the plug break the surface for a brief second before carrying on again as before.

Another angler, drawing on his past memories of similar conditions, might try a fast, steady retrieve with a big, bright tandem-bladed spinnerbait. Both tactics could catch on the same day, but on another day only the one might work. So the answer is not simply to own lots of different lures but to understand how to work them and put this into practice until you catch. Even if two anglers used the same lure, they would get differing results because the way that the lure is worked is of paramount importance. In the long term, experience will help you determine quickly which lure will work in a given situation and how to work it but this takes a long time to understand and cannot be learned from books.

I have not named any particular lures yet because what they do is more important than a manufacturer's name. Once you understand the different characteristics of lures you can then go out and choose those that fall into that category. For simplicity, I will categorize lures as plugs, spoons and spinners. Beyond these are a whole host of artificials that need to be seriously considered and provide endless scope for experimentation. Many areas overlap and hybrid lures cloud the issue even further but do not let this confuse you at this early stage. The complete range is so extensive that it goes beyond the scope of a book of this nature. Look at these other developments by all means but master the principles of the basic lure types first.

Spoons

Spoons are the simplest lure to start fishing with. They are simply an elongated and shaped strip of metal with a hook fixed at one end by means of a split ring and, at the other, a split ring and swivel attachment to which is connected the trace. There are several variations that include weed-guards and bead-eye features and some even have an extra treble fitted along their length. They vary considerably in both size and weight. Spoons are very versatile and can be fished at long range and in deep water. Normally they are cast out and retrieved at a steady pace, although in deep weed-free water it is possible to impart an irregular action into them by jerking the rod occasionally. I find the steady retrieve more productive.

Endless combinations of shapes and colouration give spoons different actions and flash patterns. When the pike are in an aggressive mood early in the season they will often take any spoon but later on they can be quite selective and it pays to have a variety of actions, sizes and colours to choose from. Spoons are also employed in the highly specialized art of trolling from a boat using down-riggers to hold the lure at a particular depth. Keeping the lure at the feeding depth can also be critical.

A Few Of My Favourite Spoons

Abu Toby, (18g black and gold)
Nilsmaster Krokodil 80, (23g perch scale pattern)
Kuusamo Professor 1H, (27g perch scale pattern)

Spinners

Spinners, as the name suggests, have a blade that rotates around a shaft as the lure is retrieved through the water. It sends out a very different signal to that of the spoon both visually and audibly. If a spoon does not work, feeding pike cannot be considered to be absent until this different presentation has been tried. Like the spoon, it can be steadily retrieved or given a jerky action to make it rise in the water and then flutter enticingly downwards.

A Few Of My Favourite Spinners

Blue Fox. Super Vibrax 4. (Silver blade)
Mepps. Aglia 5. (Brass blade)
Abu. Droppen (12g copper/red blade)

Plugs

With proper application, spoons and spinners are highly effective pike catchers. They have one snag though and that is, if you were to stop reeling, they would fall to the bottom. This can be a good tactic where there is a clean bottom but invariably there are weeds or snags to contend with. Should one wish to work a bait slowly, over snaggy terrain of rocks, weed or sunken branches, it is often a better option to use a plug. A plug is simply a fish-shaped piece of wood or plastic with trebles attached.

To the beginner, the range seems incredibly complex. Magazine articles compound the confusion by throwing all sorts of weird and strange sounding names at the reader, many of which are no longer available. Do not worry about this, as there are in actual fact only a handful of different basic types and most of the names that you hear will belong to one of them. The names are invented by the multitude of manufacturers to make their own products recognizable in a large complex market. Variations in action, colour, shape or any combination of these simply adds another name to the list of lures. I find it easiest to consider the depth that a plug works as a way of categorizing it. Variations in its attributes can then be classed under sub-headings.

Plugs Which Work on the Surface

Any plug that floats can be worked on the surface by using a very slow retrieve, but to make sure that you get the right signals to the pike, certain lures are specifically designed to work best on the top. Some will be recognized by the absence of a diving vane or lip at the front end. When they are retrieved, these lures are reluctant to dive. Instead they travel across the surface sending out many different signals depending upon their design. Some have rotating propellers or paddles that rotate and slap the water representing a small mammal in distress. The vibrations and ripple patterns that they emit are very obvious from below, especially when the surface of the water is smooth.

Some lures through a jerking action from the rod, create a popping sound to attract the attentions of predators. This type of lure is recognizable by its concave front end which helps create the sound. In skilful hands they can be made to dart, wiggle and splash in a very enticing manner. They are particularly effective over dense weed and in this situation, this may be the only practical way to catch pike. Sometimes, pike will be seen approaching from many yards away as they home in on the disturbance, creating a bow wave as they do so. This is a very exciting and rather underused technique, which is usually relegated to warmer days when pike are lying high in the water but it can be effective at other times in shallow water.

Some Favourite Surface Lures

Heddon. Lucky 13. (3¾in, ⅝oz red head pattern)
Bomber. 3T Popper. (3½in, ⅜oz black/yellow)
Repel. Buzz-n-frog. (3in, ¾oz frog coloured)

Shallow-diving plugs

By the addition of a lip or angled vane at the front end, a plug can be made to dive. The size and angle of the lip and the buoyancy of the material used determines how steeply and ultimately how deep the lure dives. Shallow divers that go down, say two yards or so, have relatively small lips. These may be adjustable to vary the depth reached. The manufacturer's stated maximum depth is related to a specific speed of retrieve and so naturally a slower speed will not take them down so far. Some plugs will dive to a given depth and then stay there quite easily as long as the retrieve speed is maintained. Others are too buoyant and are straining to shoot back towards the surface when the speed is reduced, and to my mind do not behave as naturally. These are the sort of things you need to consider when choosing a plug for your needs.

As with the surface plugs, the variation in body design is considerable. They come in an enormous variety of sizes, body shapes, colours and actions. Pike anglers will argue all day long over the merits of each type. Comparing results with other keen lure anglers is always interesting and the source of much disagreement! The variety is immense and the scope for experimentation in different waters is endless. If you are not careful you may fall into the trap of having one or two favourite patterns and using them everywhere. Whilst confidence is very important in lure fishing, it is wise to keep experimenting and a change of lure has often brought me surprising and unexpected results.

Some Favourite Shallow-Working Plugs

Nilsmaster. 12 cm. Invincible. (24g yellow perch pattern)
Cotton Cordell. Riplin Redfin. (4½in, ⅜oz shad pattern)
Rapala. Fat Rap. (2¾in, ⁷⁄₁₆oz gold/red pattern)

Deep-Diving Plugs

In the UK, these are not available in as many patterns as the shallow divers since the waters that we commonly fish are rarely much more than three or four yards deep. There are however, waters where lures that search deeper are required, such as big reservoirs, lochs and certain pits. Large, heavy spoons seem to be a popular choice in these instances. As with deep-diving plugs, they spend most of the retrieve time either sinking or rising, and do not effectively fish the required depth for very long. To reach the optimum depth quickly and then maintain it, these lures are best trolled behind a boat. These plugs are notable for their disproportionately large lips whose surface area ensures that when retrieved they overcome their buoyancy and stay down. Depths to over 20 feet may be searched with these plugs which have a good variety of size, shape and action too. By adding weight uptrace, even greater depths can be fished. They may also be used in shallower water to 'bump' the bottom and create a disturbance that might attract the attention of predators. Mud embedded in the vane is usually the sign that you have hit bottom although this fact can usually be felt when retrieving.

A Few Favourite Deep Divers

Heddon. Magnum Tadpolly. (3¾in, grey/black pattern, reaches 22 feet)
Lindy. No 7 Baitfish. (4½in, wounded perch pattern, reaches 14 feet)
Rapala. SR9 Rap. (3½in, ⁹⁄₁₆oz shad pattern, reaches 14 feet)

Sinking Plugs

Having no buoyancy these plugs sink, and the rate at which they sink depends upon the materials used in their construction. These are more difficult for a beginner to get to grips with and easier to lose. With a buoyant plug, the angler stops retrieving as soon as he feels a snag and generally the lure rises above it. With a sinker this does not happen and you are more likely to lose it. Their advantage is that they can be worked in a more natural manner as they are not forever straining to rise in the water even on a very slow retrieve. My biggest lure-caught pike came on such a lure and shortly afterwards, on another water, I lost another huge fish on it.

A Few Favourite Sinking Plugs

Rapala. Countdown. (4⅜in, ⁹⁄₁₆oz silver pattern)
Abu. Hi-Lo. (4¼in, 28 g red head pattern)
Cotton Cordell. Rattle Spot. (3in, ½oz, chrome/black)

Spinnerbaits

The last type of lure that I would like to mention is the spinnerbait. These really are a devastating lure, introduced to this country from America in recent years. They are, I suppose, a type of spinner but not in the traditional sense that we know them in the UK. On the commonest types, the hook and the blade are set on two separate arms joined together almost like an opened safety-pin. The hook is usually on the bottom and the blade on the top arm. The hook is surrounded by a multi-stranded rubber skirt, feathers or hair. The hook may be a treble or a single or sometimes both. The blade can be single or tandem and is subject to several popular shapes. The single-hook type are particularly weed-resistant as the hook is upturned preventing it from catching.

Fitting 'stinger' hooks to spinnerbaits.

They cast tremendously well and there are different sizes to allow fishing at all sorts of speeds and depths.

A Few Favourite Spinnerbaits

Lindy. Fuzz-E-Grub. (¼oz black body)
Lindy. Tandem blade (⅜oz chartreuse/orange skirt)
Lindy. Big Fin Tandem. (1oz black/white skirt)

There is no need to become easily confused by a lure with a strange name. Consider its purpose. How deep and fast is it intended to be fished? What is its action? How is it worked? What colours are available? When you have asked all these questions, ask yourself whether it could improve your results on a particular water. If it could not, forget about it, because you will never be able to afford them all!

You will note that I have listed a few of my favourites. I do not know all the lures intimately and certainly cannot afford to try them all, especially as they often come in many colour variations. The ones mentioned have been good to me on the waters that I have lure fished and are by no means the best. In time you will build up your own collection of 'catchers' but I am sure that they will be different from mine!

A book of this nature cannot delve much deeper into the highly specialized world of lure fishing. My own lure fishing for pike takes in the use of soft rubber fish, mounted on snap-tackles, which are devastatingly effective at times. From boats and overhead structures, I am finally getting to grips with 'jigs' which are simply lures which are worked up and down in the water, usually with a sharp rise and an enticingly slow fall until something grabs them. It really works! Then there is the possibility of making up hybrid lures such as plugs with rotating blades attached or spinners with rubber tails added. The permutations are endless and one could become totally absorbed in this fascinating aspect of angling.

Lure fishing is often referred to as a beginner's method; an easy way to start pike fishing. My opinion has greatly altered in the last few years. I believe that lure fishing is the most skilful aspect of pike fishing and one that pike anglers should work up to rather than begin with.

The author's late wife, Stephanie, with one of many fish caught on their trips together.

6 SEPTEMBER – ALL CHANGE

Is September late summer or early autumn? I am always unsure about this. You could argue that if it stays warm it is still summer and if it turns cold, autumn has arrived. As usual nature has a way of making the whole business quite unpredictable. Whatever the weather though, for me September marks a changing point. If I can feel that a change is in the air, I am sure that the pike can too. It is the time of year when I put thoughts of mobile and opportunist piking a little further, but not entirely, to the back of my mind and start serious preparations for the cold weather piking to come.

Proper preparation involves a great deal of ground work if the winter fishing is to run smoothly and efficiently. As usual in my fishing, little is left to chance. There is no one thing that is particularly complicated, but there are such a vast number of things to consider that the combined total of all these jobs can be quite staggering if left to the last minute. If you do not do this

Into the lion's den.

foundation work, stagnation can set in leading to disillusionment. With so many other factors working against you, at least be sure that you do not let yourself down by not making the effort.

Remember that we are now thinking ahead to much colder days when everything seems that much more difficult than it did in the comparative warmth of September. Think ahead to December. Imagine a time when temperatures are plummeting and a freeze-up is forecast. Pike will be virtually uncatchable, perhaps for weeks on end. They will probably feed so little at this time that, when the thaw comes, they will be ravenous. On many waters that I fish, these conditions often result in livebaits scoring highly against deadbaits and the man with a bin full of the former on those first days of the thaw, will usually be very successful. Will you be the one who spends his time catching livebaits or using second-rate methods when the thaw arrives, or will you arrive at the swim fully prepared and have a bonanza?

WELL PREPARED

I remember well the big freeze-up of 78/79. The cold snap was well forecast and I knew exactly what to do to be ready for when it was all over. My livebait catching water was freezing over but I spent two afternoons fishing through the remaining holes in the ice for roach until I could cast in no more. It was a prolific water and even in the coldest weather produced well on the bread punch. It was actually very enjoyable fishing even though the roach were to end up as baits. I even had proper consent from the water authority to transfer these fish and had obtained permission from the club to remove them as the pool was badly overrun with stunted fish. Gaining such consents might not be so easy to do nowadays and so you will have to weigh up the risks that you are taking by collecting baits in this way. I am in no position to recommend what you do except to say that discretion is the best policy!

In this particular case, I fished like a demon as the water area became smaller and smaller until finally there was no open water left to cast into. At least it was easy to catch the roach and this made the exercise bearable. By the time I had finished, there were almost 200 baits in my tanks, all ready for when it would be possible to pike fish again.

My storage tanks had been well prepared for storing livebaits much earlier on in the year. At the time I had two 50-gallon containers in the garage with mains-operated air pumps and all the necessary tubing and airstones. For extremely cold conditions, they were placed on polystyrene sheets and further insulation was wrapped and tied around the outside. Old coats and blankets were then covered over them. The pumps were in position ready to use and spare pumps, air lines and airstones were ready for emergencies. Lids were fitted to the tanks to make them cat-proof and to prevent baits like chub and dace from jumping out. I even had to make my air lines cat-proof as 'Old Tom' had the annoying habit of chewing the pipe and piercing it! Fitting the air line through a length of old hose-pipe prevented this. A small net was made for getting the baits out of the icy cold water which made this operation less painful.

In a fortnight of sub-zero night temperatures, dropping to as low as −16°C, only a dozen or so baits were lost. All I had to do was to check them each morning before work, break the surface ice and remove the ice that had formed on the inside walls when it got too thick. This procedure was kept up until the thaw came. It was well worth the trouble for whilst others were struggling to catch baits when the thaw came, I was piking and after a long lay-off I was having the time of my life. On the first day, against the receding ice I took fish of 15lb 6oz, 19lb 12oz and 10lb 1oz. Four further sessions over the next few days produced another thirty-five pike weighing in total 323lb. These included fourteen doubles to 19lb 9oz. I virtually had the fishing to myself. Livebaits accounted for the bulk of the fish caught. Was it worth the trouble to be prepared? Of course it was!

I hope that this illustrates that thorough preparation pays dividends. In this example, it would have been no good deciding to sort out livebait tanks and all the other refinements at the last minute. Apart from the bitter cold temperatures which makes even being outdoors unpleasant, my limited spare time had to be spent collecting bait and this was easier knowing that the tanks were set up and ready to receive them. There is such a lot to get ready, and as bait collecting is only one matter to attend to, forward thinking is essential.

As I have shown, correct preparation can affect your results tremendously. If you are serious about catching lots of pike and not settling for the odd one or two every now and again, this ground work is vital. By September, much should have been done already, especially if you have been piking through the summer.

BAIT PREPARATION

Baits are a most important aspect of piking, and I have already looked at setting up a livebait tank. Whether you livebait or not is up to you. I have never had any qualms about it and never will. There is far too much squeamishness in modern society. A great deal of thought about this matter has led me to conclude that livebaiting for pike is hardly a candidate for the shameful list of cruel and wicked things that human beings do, not only to other creatures but to each other. The decision is yours but be in no doubt that there are many piking situations that you cannot tackle efficiently without using them.

Deadbaiting is probably the most popular approach to piking at the moment and this can be devastatingly effective on many waters if carried out properly. Apart from the dozens of other considerations involved, the deadbaiter should at least get the easy part right. That is, he should have a good selection of properly prepared baits available at all times. Nipping into the supermarket on the evening before a session and seeing what is available is not the way to do it!

A well-organized pike fisherman will probably have his own bait freezer. Initially he might make use of the family food freezer but the kids will soon get fed up with the chocolate mousse

smelling of herrings! A small chest freezer, which is quite cheap to run, can be picked up for a very reasonable price if you look around for a second-hand one that might be a little tatty on the outside. It is best kept in the garage, out of the family's way and can be used not only for deadbaits but for other baits such as hemp, bread and sweetcorn. To fill any large gaps, family food that is well wrapped such as bread can be used to pack it out and reduce running costs.

It seems quite straight forward to buy baits and put them in the freezer ready for use. Unfortunately, it is a lot more involved than that and a system of bait management is necessary if you wish to avoid getting into a confusing mess. To be properly prepared, you will want a full range of baits ready to use at short notice.

A look at the contents of my own freezer will give an idea of what I mean. I like to have both

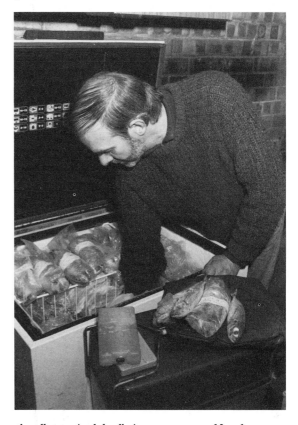

A well-organized deadbait storage system. Note freezer box, coolbag and ice blocks.

sea fish baits and freshwater fish baits available. The sea fish normally include the reliable favourites such as herrings, mackerel, smelts and sardines. In addition, I might have scad, gurnard, goat fish and sprats if I can get them at the right size and quality. The freshwater fish normally include roach, perch, dace, chub and bream but other fish of the right size like small carp and tench are acquired if I can get them. In the freshwater category too come trout and eels, which are both firm favourite baits of mine. Exactly what you stock depends to a large extent on what you can get, on what works on your waters and the proposed future usage. It becomes more complicated if you wish to have a selection of buoyant baits amongst some of these species. Then you might wish to flavour some, not to mention colouring some with food dyes. Some baits will receive a combination of these treatments. You will also want to know which are fresh baits and which have been brought back from a session and re-frozen. Even if you start with a tidy, well-organized freezer, things can soon change when you are looking for a few red, buoyant mackerel tails at five o'clock in the morning and you are still half asleep!

It is very important to pack and label everything carefully. Every bait I prepare is frozen individually and wrapped tightly with cling film or in a plastic bag to prevent dehydration. Packs are then made up of six baits which are put into larger plastic bags, wrapped tightly and bound with masking tape. On this I write exactly what the pack contains. A typical label might read: six smelts(B)/orange/used/fair(Island). You will use your own codes of course but this, to me, signifies that within that pack are six smelts packed with buoyancy and dyed orange. They have been used once but are still in fair condition and destined for use at the Island pit (an easy water where the pike will take anything and top quality bait is never necessary). Every now and again, it is necessary to have a clear-out and baits that I know will never be used are usually dumped in a water where I know that the pike will benefit from a free meal. Otherwise they are used to experiment with groundbaiting or pre-baiting.

The beauty of owning a decent-sized bait freezer is that you are always prepared to handle a load of bait should you suddenly acquire it. You never know when this will be. The obvious time is when you see a bargain in the fish market or someone tells you that they can supply cheap bait in bulk. Alternatively, you may suddenly find that all your livebaits are dead for some reason and you unexpectedly have a load of deadbaits on your hands! Sometimes you might have a stroke of luck as I did on Bough Beech Reservoir after my last day of the March 1992 sessions. The rules there state that no dead fish should be thrown in to the reservoir and so all anglers brought their expired trout livebaits back to the boatyard. I happened to mention that I would be taking mine home to freeze them and before I knew it, I was showered with unwanted trout deadbaits from other anglers. That night I prepared almost a hundred baits for the freezer. With only two days of the season left I put them to good use on two local waters and took a stack of pike including eleven doubles to 20lb 5oz. Thanks lads!

TACKLE CHECK LIST

If you are piking all the year round, as I am, most of your tackle is probably in good order. If not, it needs checking over, partly to see whether it needs tidying up and partly to ensure that you have everything you will need for the waters that you intend to fish in the months ahead. Most serious pike anglers have a pretty good idea where and how they intend to fish each season and, for me, sitting down and planning the campaign ahead is one of the pleasures of pike fishing. In doing this planning, whether on paper or simply in your mind, you can determine whether there are any shortcomings in your tackle and what you intend to do about it. You might, for example, be thinking of tackling a big reservoir using long-range drifting tactics from the bank. Will your rods be capable of setting hooks at a hundred and fifty yards range? Do you own drifting floats and line grease? Do you have spare floats? You are bound to lose a few! Do you have

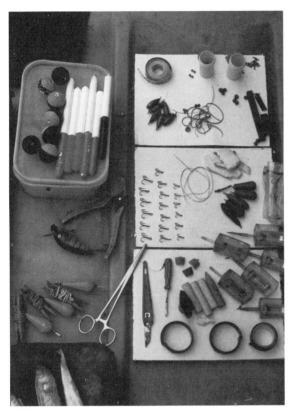

My tackle box emptied out.

a pair of binoculars to keep track of floats at range? Have you a tube to carry the float stems in to prevent them from being bent and damaged? These are the sort of questions you must ask yourself now, rather than the evening before you go fishing.

Go through all your tackle and make sure everything is in good condition and in good supply. Here is a typical check list of basic bits and pieces that I might have in my rucksack. Bear in mind that each item will be backed up with spares kept either in the car or tackle room.

Line

If in any doubt about it at all, throw it away and start the winter with new spools. Buy the best you can afford and never use less than 12lb breaking strain. Apart from my normal spools I have others which are permanently greased for drifting or for circumstances where I want the line to stay off the bottom.

Wire

There are many good multi-strand wires on the market. My favourite has always been Berkeley 20lb breaking strain and I have never yet found any reason to change to another type. Buying it on 100m spools is most economical.

Livebaiting Floats

I rarely use anything other than 1¼in and 1½in drilled and painted poly balls. They are perfectly adequate for sensible-sized baits on both rivers and still waters. They are used for paternostering, trotting, trolling and medium range drifting. They are so cheap and last so long that it is worth having at least half a dozen in your bag.

Deadbaiting Floats

The seven-inch long balsa stick floats that I make myself are all I ever use. Some have orange tips for blue water conditions and some have black tips for white water or sunny conditions. They are non-self-cocking and, again, I always like to have half a dozen with me. My latest ones are reversible with orange at one end and black at the other.

Beads

It used to be difficult finding beads with small holes in them but nowadays they are readily available. The packet of 100 Gardener 3mm diameter beads that I bought about ten years ago has only just run out! I transfer them to a plastic transparent film container with a reliable snap top and they get used over and over again.

Stop-Knots

For the last twenty years or so I have been quite happy with using fine elastic bands for stop-knots and always keep a dozen or so in my box. When tied carefully with a simple granny knot, they will not slip, provided that the line is not greasy, and certainly will not damage the line as other materials do. I have never been happy in this respect with nylon and power-gum knots which need a lot of care to use safely.

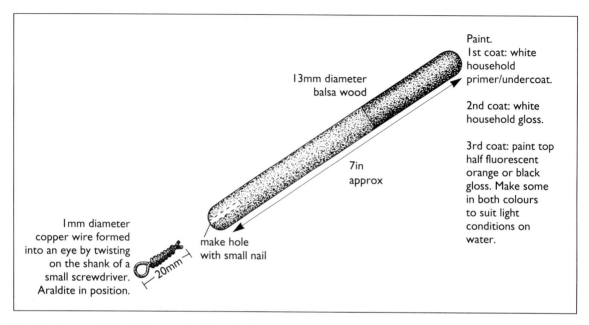

13mm diameter
balsa wood

Paint.
1st coat: white
household
primer/undercoat.

2nd coat: white
household gloss.

3rd coat: paint top
half fluorescent
orange or black
gloss. Make some
in both colours
to suit light
conditions on
water.

7in
approx

1mm diameter
copper wire formed
into an eye by twisting
on the shank of a
small screwdriver.
Araldite in position.

20mm

make hole
with small nail

Simple, cheap and effective home-made balsa deadbaiting float.

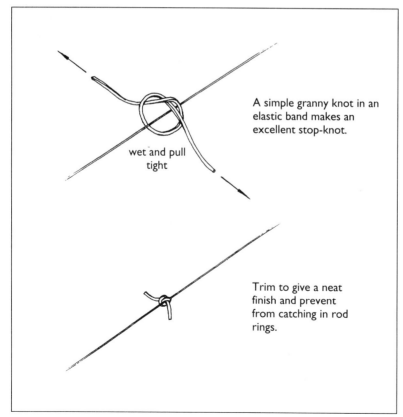

A simple granny knot in an
elastic band makes an
excellent stop-knot.

wet and pull
tight

Trim to give a neat
finish and prevent
from catching in rod
rings.

*Making a stop knot from a piece of
rubber band.*

Swivels

I think that the Berkeley 50lb breaking strain swivels take a lot of beating for most pike fishing situations and I rarely use anything else. When using 15lb line and 30lb wire, I normally uprate to 65lb b.s. swivels. These too are transferred to a transparent film container. An important point worth noting is that I segregate new and used swivels. The used ones are kept in a separate tub and each has a small length of either nylon or wire left on it to show what was previously tied to

it. The point of this is that wire can damage swivels by scoring the surface and when nylon is tied to them on a later occasion, it can break very easily. I had a lot of trouble with knots and often blamed the line itself before I realized what was actually happening. Black swivels are best so that you can clearly see whether this damage has occurred but when tying up traces in poor light this might not be obvious so I make sure by using the procedure described. If in any doubt, throw them away.

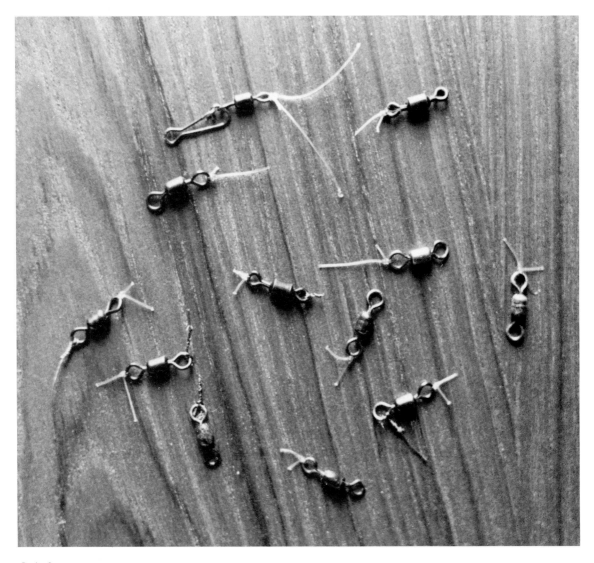

Swivel management.

Treble Hooks

In addition to my ready-made-up traces, I only find it necessary to take about a dozen extra hooks in sizes 6, 8 and 10. Using good quality hooks and fishing sensibly means that I get through very few hooks in the course of a season. When not in use, keep them dry and sharpen them if necessary before re-using them.

Swan Shot

I find that about thirty lead-free shot will be adequate and keep them in a film container.

Leads

Again, I only carry what I will need as they are, obviously, heavy items. Usually there are six ¾oz leads for paternostering and six 2oz leads for legering or putting into a swimfeeder to give it extra weight. If I am going to a particularly snaggy place then I will put in a few more. I can never see the point of carrying dozens of heavy leads as some anglers do.

Swimfeeders

At times, it pays to have all the attraction power that you can get. With this in mind I carry half a dozen large feeders with the holes well opened up to aid release of scent from mashed fish. Always wash them out after use as the smell can be unbearable!

Line Grease

This is essential for greasing the line when using drifting tactics or keeping line above weed or snags with long-range, float-fished deadbaits.

Hook Guards

These can be very useful, especially when moving swims or travelling with made-up rods in the motor or in the boat as they prevent the frustration caused by flying trebles getting caught up on everything in sight. I carry about half a dozen or so for this purpose.

Forceps

I have an eight-inch pair which have yet to meet a pike that they cannot handle with ease. I see no

need for those enormous ones that I often notice in use. It may seem a minor point but if you keep the teeth clean, they grip so much better. It is surprising just how much they get gummed up with mud, slime and fish scales.

Wire Cutters

I now only carry a five-inch pair. They are only used for cutting wire and nylon. The use of long-handled pliers and cutters for removing hooks from pike should be a thing of the past.

Balsa Wood Sticks

I carry about half a dozen, two-inch sticks of 8mm diameter balsa for inserting into deadbaits to make them buoyant. I tie such baits onto the trace so that nothing ever gets the chance to swallow them should a bait come adrift when casting or playing a fish.

Polystyrene

A small amount of polystyrene, in the form of broken ceiling tiles, is carried as an alternative to the balsa sticks. The same rules of tying on baits prepared in this way still apply. With polystyrene it is easier to make small adjustments. There are other materials on the market specifically made for this purpose but I am quite happy with what I use.

Needle and Cotton

A large darning needle and a few yards of fine braided nylon or kitchen string have a multitude of uses. The main one is for tying on buoyant baits as previously mentioned. They are also useful for sewing up the ends of half baits, usually after inserting buoyant material but also occasionally to make baits more streamlined so that they cast better. Other uses are for repairing clothes, nets and sacks in an emergency. These are well worth carrying for what little room they take up.

Oil Stone

This is essential for keeping hooks needle sharp and especially on gravel pits and rocky-bottomed waters.

A variety of run indicators. From left to right: homemade drop-off alarm; sleeve bobbins; drop-off sight bobbin; optonic, simple polyball drop-off indicator; E.T. double 'back-biter' alarm.

Run Indicators

The ones that I will take depend upon where and how I am fishing. If at all possible I prefer to watch a float simply because I enjoy doing so. When I leger or use a sunken-float rig, I like the simplicity of a drop-off sight bobbin and this might be used in conjunction with an optonic if it is not easy to see my rods due to difficult banks. For long waits, I use back-biters. I have two types: the popular E. T. type or home-made ones built for me by Steve Bown, an electrical engineer from the Midlands. They are also used when night fishing or at other times when I might either fall asleep or be distracted from my rods. An audible continuous alarm is essential in those instances that require an instant response in order to prevent deep hooking. On a long session, it is wise to carry spare batteries.

Tape Measure

I use a lightweight one from a sewing kit. My interest goes far beyond just catching pike and you can learn a lot from their vital statistics.

Small Screwdriver

This is essential for changing batteries on optonics and backbiters.

Optonic Key

This instrument is essential to stop optonics from coming loose on windy days. What would I do without it?

Electrical Tape

A small roll is carried and is useful for all sorts of minor temporary repairs such as securing rod rings or reels. I have even taped my rods to the rests in really evil weather but the John Roberts rod-rests that grip the rod tightly have now eliminated this.

Craft Knife

Fitted with a very sharp blade and protector, the craft knife is very useful for making a neat job of cutting up and trimming deadbaits. It is also useful for puncturing deadbaits to release body fluids when necessary.

Traces

While I think that trace-tidies are an excellent idea I find them too bulky for my fishing. I simply coil up my traces and slip them into small plastic sleeves. They can easily be carried in my pocket in this way. The type and number that I carry depends upon where and how I am fishing. I have plenty of traces made up at home and grab the ones that I will need for the session. Usually I have a selection of one- and two-treble rigs available in sizes 6, 8 and 10. I am usually most happy fishing for big pike with 6s and only go smaller when I have no choice, which is very rare. While I am fishing, I use any spare time available to make up new traces to replace those used in the session.

Radio

It gets quite lonely when you spend a lot of time on your own in remote places and a radio is good company. It is a good way of keeping alert to approaching bad weather, especially when out in the boat.

Torch

A small torch is essential for starting and finishing in the dark or tying on traces and unhooking fish in darkness. If I am out in the boat at night, I always carry another large, powerful and reliable torch for emergencies.

This is only a brief check list that suits my own fishing. You will have one to suit your approach and requirements. However, it should give you some idea of how much preparation is necessary if sessions are to run smoothly and efficiently.

RIVER PIKE FROM A BOAT

September is not just a time for dull preparatory work – far from it. There is some good piking to be had in this month and, believe me, September pike can really jump and fight. I have had some terrific sport on pits, drains and reservoirs at this time of year but the most enjoyable September piking that I can remember was in the late seventies and early eighties on the River Severn. In an earlier chapter, I described the tactics for piking of the big river weirs. Now I would like to describe fishing in the main river itself both from the bank and from a boat.

When I first tackled the Severn many years ago, very few contemporary pike anglers had considered the possibility of rivers as prime pike waters. Subsequent experiences have shown that there is enormous potential for catching pike in rivers and river pike are now seriously pursued by those in the know. It is not just the sluggish rivers that hold pike, for they can be found in quite swiftly flowing water.

I clearly remember reading an article on river pike published back in the late sixties which stated that 95 per cent of pike would be located within a few feet of the bank. Believing this to be true, I started fishing the Severn in this way and caught quite a few nice fish. I also fished large slacks and on the edges of the faster water. Initially, my results were not too fantastic but what a place to fish for pike. The atmosphere of the river valley at daybreak is one of real peace and tranquillity. With the mist rising from the swirling surface, mink scurry from bank to bank and kingfishers speed by like darts. The Severn is very special to me. By mid-morning though, holiday cruisers chug past, pleasure anglers line the banks and the magic disappears.

My interest in the river escalated dramatically when I heard that a nineteen-pounder had been caught from the area where I was fishing. To my surprise it had been taken on a bait trotted through with the heavy flow. I would not be in the least bit surprised now, but at that time, as I was far less experienced, it seemed an unlikely prospect when there was a huge piece of slack

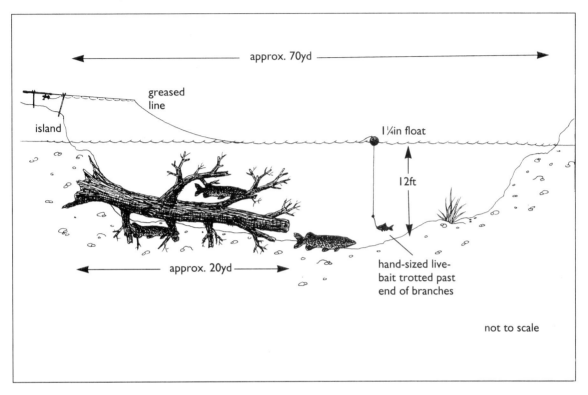

The Sunken Tree Swim at Tewkesbury on the River Severn.

water nearby. Subsequent experience has proved to me that pike will often be caught in heavily flowing and turbulent water but that is not to say that they prefer to be there. It seems to me that they will enter disturbed water of this nature when it suits them to do so for feeding but for most of the time they are lying nearby in a sheltered position where the flow has no effect on them at all.

Writers of the past were right in so much as the margins and slacks are places where river pike like to lie. They like the quiet life when not actively feeding but practice has shown me that this shelter is provided in many other very unlikely spots. In the swim that the nineteen-pounder came from, there was an enormous sunken tree on the river bed. It was a huge obstruction stretching nearly a third of the way across the river and I was later to find it to be an incredible holding feature for pike. Debris that built up on its submerged branches was ideal for providing a respite from the flow for the great numbers of big pike that inhabited the area.

My first session in the swim was a real eye opener as until then I knew nothing of what was under the water. The swim was located at the tip of a large island and this obviously restricted where I could fish it from. Straight away I was snagging up and I had to find some way of preventing this. Eventually, after working out just how far across the river this great obstruction reached, I decided to cast beyond it with a trotted livebait and hoped that some of the pike would be outside the lair. This involved quite a long cast and not one that I would like to subject a bait to normally as it would not last very long.

After a little trial and error, a take finally came and in dealing with it, I used a procedure that I can honestly say, never lost me a single fish as a result of snagging up. The hooks were set, but I only maintained the minimum pressure required to keep them on. The pike went out into the flow and

*My standard 42in landing net. It has a large mesh and a soft bottom
section. Note the alternative short handle used for boat fishing.*

A Severn 'twenty' taken from the sunken tree.

drifted off downstream. With about 80 yards of line out, and the pike well away from the snag, I reconnected with it. I was able to persuade it to fight it out below the tree and then in the backwater to my right.

I am one of those happy souls who likes the pike to try and pull my arm from its socket when I am playing one. I like pike to tear away on unstoppable runs and send the clutch screaming. This one, like most of the Severn pike in summer and early autumn, did not disappoint me and, after a good struggle, she was netted. I have an eye for detail when it comes to pike and I instantly recognized that pike as the one that I had caught there on my last visit in one of the traditional near-bank swims further downstream. Still unaware of the potential of the swim, I was left

wondering if such a recapture meant that there were very few pike in the area. Little did I know!

As I returned the pike, I realized that I had been lucky in finding a new swim but doubly lucky on the day because the stretch that I usually fished, across the other side of the backwater, was being pegged for a match and I would have been moved on anyway. About an hour after the match had started, I got my second take, a modest fish of 8lb 10oz, this time taken on a live hand-sized perch trotted just beyond the submerged tree again. This aroused the interest of some of the matchmen and I had to put up with the usual comments about my 42-inch net such as 'After sharks, mate?' and so on.

Shortly afterwards while using the same tactics with a live roach I was away again but this time

John Sidley and the author with one of many good catches of Severn pike.

into a real stubborn fighter. After bringing it right back up the river and into the back swim, it kited through two or three of the match pegs and then proceeded to head straight into the tree. There was nothing I could do about it. As it went in I could feel the chafing and grating of nylon against wood and feared for the worst. Inch by inch, and expecting a break at any second, it came out and I managed to keep it at the rod tip for three or four minutes. By now, several of the matchmen had left their pegs to watch. After ten minutes of pulling and tugging there was quite an audience waiting to see what it was and I heard talk of salmon and barbel. With the power of the fish, the pull of the current and the fact that I was stuck in silt on the edge of a dangerous river the fun turned into a nightmare. Four or five times

she was almost in the net but I just could not manage those last few vital inches.

When the pike did finally go in, I had recovered over 30 yards of badly damaged line but the 11lb Sylcast had held well. I was quite surprised to hear a great cheer go up from the matchmen as I netted her but it was not as loud as the one going on inside of me! At 20lb 2oz I was overjoyed as I caught fewer twenties then than I do today. It was a short and fat fish, very untypical of any other Severn pike that I had caught before or have caught since. As the matchmen dispersed, one shouted across for the weight. Misunderstanding what I had said, he turned to a friend to inform him that I had just had a twenty-two! Later that night in the local pub, I am told, it had grown by another five pounds or so!

Having worked out how to fish the swim, I naturally returned there again as soon as possible. Unfortunately, I was not the only person after that swim and a certain young man from Birmingham named John Sidley was following up the reports there too. Luckily, on this occasion, I just pipped John to the swim and he had to be content with fishing the only other decent swim available, in the weirpool. This time I was fully prepared, armed with plenty of baits. It was a day to savour. The sun shone all day and the gentle breeze carried the unique smell of the Severn Valley in its path. The lock-keeper's goats ate my sandwiches again but I had neither time nor desire to care. Pike came steadily throughout the day on the successful trotted livebait tactics and I ended with a very sore right arm after netting nine wonderful fish including a brace of seventeens and other doubles. As fast as I netted each pike, all I wanted was to do it all over again. They say that some days you will remember all of your life. For me, this was one of them.

Once I had sorted out the killing method, it was so easy. The bait was set about two feet off the bottom, although at this time of year I doubt whether that was critical. The line was well-greased to allow it to move down the flow with the bait and to prevent it from snagging on some of the branches which come within a foot of the surface in places. Three or four swan shot on the trace then keeps the livebait down. Because of the risk of snagging, I only used one size 6 treble in the lip of the bait and this gave me no problems. The pike must have really been hammering into the baits as witnessed by the globules of water shooting in the air as the float slammed under each time. The sport continued like this for several more weekends and many fish to 19lb 4oz were taken but then the river became unfishable because of the autumn rains, which made the flow just too strong for me to contend with.

My friends and I had experienced brilliant sport but were obviously making hard work of it from the bank. We were only tapping a small part of the potential of the river, but steep tree-lined banks made life very difficult and limited our options. This all changed in following seasons when I put a boat on the river and this really is the only way to fish effectively for pike on such a water. Boat fishing for pike on big rivers is fraught with problems and dangers but the pleasures outweigh the risks involved.

The way the boat is prepared for river fishing is described in the chapter on weirpool piking. After fishing the weir, tackling the main river is a lot simpler and also far less nerve-racking! The beauty of the boat is that, with the aid of the current, a bait can cover a great deal of water for little effort on the angler's part. No more long casting and damaging valuable livebaits! There is no point in casting the bait across the river and stunning it. The best thing to do is just drop it over the side and it will then last for ages. When the swim is exhausted, lift the anchor, move across a few yards and trot a fresh strip of water. If you keep quiet in the boat, and raise and lower the anchor carefully, it is quite surprising how many takes come as soon as the bait is dropped overboard.

Although the river may seem quite even from the surface, the bottom contours are very varied and as in any water there will be features that attract pike to them for shelter and as ambushing points. On this particular stretch of the river there were only four or five reliable places where a pike could be expected and other apparently similar swims rarely, if ever, held pike. Sometimes a particular feature was the obvious explanation for the presence of pike but at other times there was no definite reason why pike should be in residence. We decided that it would obviously pay us to explore every inch of the river and this was easily possible from a boat. From now on we would catch many more pike than from the bank and for far less effort.

Trotting livebaits was probably the most devastating tactic from the boat. Sink and draw tactics did catch fish but nowhere near as many. Most times, the fishing was quite leisurely and relaxing and fish were obliging as long as river conditions were reasonable. There were times, however, when the pike were in a difficult mood and tactics needed to be varied if any were to be caught at all.

Of course, you cannot expect pike to feed all day and every day and at times they are content to lie hard on the bottom awaiting the next urge to feed. They are not prepared to move far for a bait nor chase it and need it placed right on the nose. In another chapter I mention trolling overdepth to achieve this. On a river I use a similar ploy by trotting overdepth. I set the float as much as three feet over depth and put extra shot on the trace. The bait moves very slowly down the river and is held back against the current but stays hard on the bottom. This means that eventually my bait will literally hit the pike on the head if they are in the line that I am trotting. Often they were and by continually varying this line, I took many bonus fish when all else failed. At other times, pike were in the top layer of water and the deep-fished baits went untouched. You soon learn whether this is so by occasionally holding baits back against the flow and letting them rise and fall at different depths. Some of the takes are spectacular when the pike grab the baits from the surface. Magical fishing!

Due to the dangers that are waiting for the unsuspecting when boat fishing on a river, every move needs to be carried out slowly and carefully. One operation that can become quite hair-raising at times is netting a lively fish in a heavy flow. With a friend to help, as anywhere else, it is not too difficult but on your own, it can be a nightmare. On a still water you put the net in the water and guide the fish towards it. On a river things are a little different and if you put the net in the water it is quickly washed away! This being the case you have to wait until the pike is beaten and then try to slip the net under it. That would not be so bad if river pike gave up as easily as that, but they do not, and even if they did, the current would be trying to sweep them away. With a heavy wind blowing up the river valley, you have the makings of a very frustrating exercise. With practice you learn a few tricks that make it easy. A net with a large mesh definitely helps as it is less affected by the current. I had so much trouble with the pressure of water breaking drawstrings that I made one from a piece of strong nylon cord and that did the trick. My boat-fishing landing net-handle is made of strong aluminium tube and is only three feet long so as not to get in the way. Netting the fish from the back of the boat might seems to be the best approach but is often difficult as the pike will sometimes hold on the surface in the flow just out of reach.

The whole business of netting needs to be approached with confidence and this starts with knowing that the pike is cleanly hooked and is not likely to drop off when the pressure is applied to finally net it. By using sensibly sized livebaits, say up to eight inches or so, and suitable rigs, you can be confident from the start. Bigger baits often see fish dropping off through poor hook holds and the consequent problems in timing the strike. The best technique is to beat the fish and get it to the surface a short distance upstream of where you intend to net it. Use the flow to sweep it into the net which is sunk at the last second. Perhaps one day you will try it for yourself and see how tricky it can be after winching them in on stillwaters.

Make the most of the sunshine in September for very soon, all will change!

7 OCTOBER – ALL SYSTEMS GO?

THE TRADITIONAL START

For most anglers, 1st October marks the start of their pike fishing season. Anglers like myself will often point out that these people have missed some of the best piking available by leaving it until now. But, then again, if you have not fished for pike since 14th March, as many do not, then it is certainly worth looking forward to. I suppose for the traditional pike angler, 1st October is looked forward to in much the same way that the tench fisher looks forward to the misty dawn start on 16th June. I would not try to convince anyone to do otherwise. All I know is that all-year-round piking suits me and the other species are fitted in when the whim takes me. Yet, even to me, October does still have a magic about it that, I am sure, inspires even the keenest pikers to step up their efforts.

It would be convenient to be able to generalize about a typical start to the so-called 'pike season' but I have seen enough starts to know that there is no such thing. In recent years we had just got used to summers seemingly extending into October with still, warm sunny days when suddenly, in the October of 1992 we were faced with the most windy, dull and miserable October that I could remember for many years. One thing that has been consistent is that I have enjoyed good piking in both conditions.

In October we are seeing the nights starting to get colder, damper and longer and I tend to think of pike now following a natural instinct to prepare for the potential hard times ahead that must surely come as winter draws nearer. The only way that they can do this is to feed heavily and build up their bodily reserves and so I have found that October can be an excellent month for catching pike on most waters.

If anything, I prefer the type of weather where the warm days extend into October and in brilliant sunshine I have enjoyed some fabulous piking. The more sun we get the better, I say! There is plenty of wind, rain and cold to come in the months ahead. What is more, I have often had the fishing all to myself. A large proportion of pikers are cold-weather starters, preferring to carry on fishing for the summer species until the weather breaks. What a boon it is to pike anglers that waters far and wide are now stuffed with a fairly easy-to-catch big fish species, i.e. the carp! If only a quarter of the nation's carp-crazy anglers turned their attention to the alternative big fish that the pike is, it is doubtful whether many waters could take the pressure and pike stocks would suffer. Thank goodness too that winter carp fishing is now recognized as a serious proposition and a lot of big fish men keep out of the piker's way by bivvying up behind bolt-rigs no matter how cold it gets.

BREATHING SPACE

I would recommend that you make the most of the breathing space, early in October, before other pikers start to fish seriously again. It is possible to get three or four weeks' fishing with little competition from others on many waters. In the autumn of 1992 I did just that and in the first few weeks took sixty-six pike to over 27lb from a variety of waters. I barely saw another pike angler casting a bait.

Should the October weather be sunny and calm, one would think it unlikely that pike would be very active, but they often are, and on all sorts of waters too. Where to fish can actually be quite a problem in October as virtually everywhere fishes well. I can think of dozens of pits, drains, rivers and reservoirs that I would like to pike fish in this month if I could only fit them all in. The big bonus is that October fish are lean and power ful and still full of energy. Expect some memorable fights but bear in mind that, with lots of weed still about, really strong tackle will be needed. Gravel-pit pike, especially, will weed you up and because of the way that they fight in October you will find that there is little that you can do to stop them.

For most piking, I would not insist on really expensive lines if you do not do a lot of pike fishing but under these conditions you must use a line that has the strength and abrasion-resistance qualities that will cope. October, being such a good month for piking, is probably as good a time as any to tackle some of the really big waters which can become real gruellers later on in the winter. They will usually fish well for far less effort in the early autumn.

Distraction

Despite this being such a good month for piking. I have missed out on a good deal of action due to another toothy predator – the zander. This happens to be my favourite and most successful zander month too. Much zandering is about piking as well and some nice fish of both species can be caught with a little careful planning.

EFFECT OF SUMMER PIKING

Should you decide to start piking this month, there is something important to bear in mind which could save you a little disappointment and a lot of heartache. Find out if you can if the water you are going to tackle has been pike fished earlier on in the summer and, if so, to what extent. There are waters here and there that take a real hammering in the summer and if you are an October starter you may not realize that this has happened. I try not to give a water any real pressure in the summer months, much preferring occasional short sessions using mobile tactics. I

do not believe that the odd angler doing this does any harm to the pike stocks, provided they are handled properly, of course. On the other hand, a concerted approach by a number of capable anglers using multi-rod tactics can do a lot of damage, albeit unintentionally. In fact some waters have been ruined by such actions.

There are things to consider that cause this to happen. In warm weather, pike wolf baits down very rapidly. What is more they fight like hell and get stuck in the abundance of weed growth that will be about. Casualties can and do occur due to deep hooking and excessive tiring of the fish. Mortalities are almost inevitable. When October comes around and the summer pikers have moved on, the casual pike angler will be fishing for reduced stocks and those still left will be very wary after their summer ordeal. At best, the piking will be only mediocre. Now compare this to the situation on a water that has been largely left alone since the previous winter. By contrast, runs there would tend to be more regular and certainly more confident.

GRAVEL PIT PIKE

It would be easy to find many issues to discuss about pike fishing on any type of water during this month but I will be limiting this chapter to gravel pits. In describing my approach to these waters in October, a great many of the points made will be relevant to other stillwaters too and here and there I will refer to them. In this chapter I will describe setting up, tackle rigs and baits for these waters but I want you to realize the most important aspect of catching big pit pike. They must be in the water that you are fishing. This sounds obvious but inexperienced anglers live in an innocent world where they believe everything they hear is true and think that there are unknown big pike waiting to be caught everywhere. This is not true. You can have the best bait and tackle in the world but you cannot catch pike that are not there. Success has to start with being in the right place. This information is not easy to come by, but you must seek it out.

Choosing Pits

When faced with a large choice of pits, how do you know which ones you should concentrate on? A few years ago I was faced with this very problem. When I moved my home to South Lincolnshire, I purposely located myself in an area abundant in water, including drains, rivers and gravel pits. My main interest lay in the drain fishing for both pike and zander. Already knowing the drains intimately, as a result of driving across from Birmingham to fish them for fifteen years, I was soon catching plenty of fish.

I then started to take an interest in the gravel pits. I did not get too excited about them at first, having previously fished other gravel pits around the country, without particular success. I had, wrongly, come to the conclusion that gravel pits were uninteresting places to fish and were not for me. That was one of the biggest mistakes that I have ever made. By not following up pit pike fishing at an earlier stage, I have probably robbed myself of endless chances of big pike. On my way to fish various drains and rivers, I have passed within striking range of many pits that, I now realize, were a much better prospect for a big pike than the places to which I was spending a long time travelling.

Looking back at the pits that I *did* fish, I had made some bad choices. Many were awful places to fish and to look at. The water in some was coloured and the banks were often difficult to negotiate, being strewn with concrete blocks and old cables. Most produced very few runs for me, although my friends and I did take a few high doubles and low twenties. These were no consolation for the difficult, uninteresting fishing we had had.

Having since spent six years fishing gravel pits, almost exclusively, I can sum up my failure quite easily. I did not understand pits or pit pike! I cannot assume to know it all now but I know enough to realize that I fished the wrong pits, the wrong places on those pits, the wrong times and the wrong methods. No wonder I did not catch much! For me, rivers and drains had been an easier option but I am glad that I have now come to terms with one of the most important aspects of piking.

So, how do you start to fish an area rich in gravel pits of all shapes and sizes? In my area alone, there are over 50 pits of varying sizes and states of maturity. I do not think that these are any better or any worse than those elsewhere, and from talking to other anglers it seems that I have got a good cross section of different situations. The first thing to do when beginning to fish a new area is get an Ordnance Survey map and note all the pits within the area you wish to consider. Throughout the Midlands and the south and east of England there are many vast complexes and waters are being dug out at an incredible rate to feed the construction industry. Most anglers in these areas will be within striking range of such waters. The next thing to note is that there will probably be some pits that are so new that they are not even on the map yet. These are often the ones to watch! Pits regularly turn up good pike, sometimes enormous pike, quite early on in their existence, and should never be dismissed out of hand. Pits of only five or six years of age can turn up pike over 20lb.

Having studied the map, visit each and every pit and, if possible, walk around them. Take a few photographs for reference if you like. Try to ascertain who owns the water and try and talk to anyone there, preferably anglers, about the water itself and the fish it contains. Find out how old it is, how it has been stocked and what pike fishing has been carried out there. Do not expect a lot of the facts that you gather to be very accurate or even true. Anglers pass on a lot of hearsay and sometimes tell lies to put you off from fishing their water. Whatever information you glean, it is a foundation to build upon.

When I carried out this exercise, I soon realized that there were very few places where I could actually fish. Many waters are strictly private. Some are leased for other water sports, for trout fisheries or nature reserves. Some still belong to the excavation companies. If this is the case, there will be very little known about the pike fishing potential of these waters so one has to find out for oneself. In most areas there will be a few specialist anglers, like myself, who have made a point of getting to grips with most of their local

I have caught this gravel pit twenty-pounder three times on different buoyant deadbaits.

fishing in one way or another but you are unlikely to get them to talk about specific waters. They would be stupid to give away the fruits of their labours.

Given the task of getting to grips with so many pits, as I was, I did not expect to do it over night. There was obviously several years work to do and the way to go about it was to do it methodically. If you are in this situation, realize that there will be a lot of blanks but also a lot of surprises, so, above all, enjoy the search for pike. The best thing I found to eliminate any confusion was to list each and every pit, no matter how small it might be. I only crossed it off the list when I was certain that it held no interest for me. A water is occasionally put back onto the list should something happen to change its status such as a stocking with unwanted pike from a trout water or improvement in the pike fishing. Nothing stands still on these pits and you must keep your eyes and ears open.

Naturally you will, first of all, fish where it is possible to get permission. Where other anglers are piking, make friends with them and exchange information. Tell them about the pike you catch there and they will usually reciprocate. On small to medium-sized pits you will soon find that you recognize recaptures and it does not take long to build up a picture of the big pike present. You might know the sort of thing I mean. For example, you arrive and someone informs you that the 24lb fish with the yellow spot on the belly was out yesterday. Do not disregard these known fish especially if you have never caught them yourself. When you are sure that you have caught the larger fish present in a pit, you will have to decide when to move on. There could easily be a few seasons' fishing to get to grips with these waters and some might prove harder than you think. This might be due to low pike density or their vast acreage or simply because someone else keeps catching them!

The thirty-pounder taken from under the bailiff's nose.

The next phase starts to get more interesting for you are entering the unknown. One by one, make attempts to get permission to fish the private waters. It is always worth asking and if you go about it in the right way you would be surprised at the co-operation you can get. It is not sensible to telephone the owner when he might be settled down by the television and saying to him, 'Any chance of fishing your pit mate?' It does not work! Find out why the pit is not fished and find an angle round it. Send a clearly worded introductory letter explaining your interest. Offer to bailiff the water or do some bank maintenance in exchange for permission to pike fish.

On many waters, the owners just do not want you there or are not even prepared to discuss the matter with you. Some can even be rude and nasty. The only way that you will ever fish these waters is to wait until they change hands and try again or, to be quite blunt, poach them. That is

for your conscience alone to wrestle with. In my own particular area, poaching is a way of life, often carried out with the precision of an S.A.S. exercise. In the main, it is done discreetly and sensibly. Nothing is damaged or spoilt and no-one, other than those concerned, even knows what goes on. The decision is yours!

The Nature of Pits
What can you expect when you finally get down to pike fishing these pits? Sizes will vary quite a bit and beginners would be unwise to tackle large pits of over fifty acres unless there are popular well defined areas where pike are known to be caught. Pits will vary immensely in their physical nature. Some will be shallow and some deep. Some will be cloudy and some will be gin clear. The majority in my area are very clear. Where they are clear and shallow, up to 15 feet or so, weed growth will normally be prolific. This will

be your biggest nightmare until you learn to get to grips with it.

Depths vary depending upon the depth of the excavated gravel seam. This will vary in different areas. Typically there is a yard or so of top soil, beneath which is from two to seven yards of sand and gravel. Sometimes pits are even deeper where clay has been removed from below the gravel. There are two distinctive types of pit too. The older pits have a tendency to be irregular in shape with steep, crumbling banks. They are often endowed with islands and bars where spoils have just been dumped in anywhere after the pit has been worked out. These sometimes become very picturesque as they mature and are often very pleasant places to fish. Occasionally, they become eyesores with difficult banks for anglers to fish from. Bear in mind though that physical appearance has no bearing whatsoever on what kind of fish are in the water and it is easy to get carried away just because a pit looks good.

Modern regulations insist that worked-out pits should be landscaped, which means that newer pits are beginning to look very natural. The standard practice now is to use the underlying clay to line the banks at an angle of about 45 degrees to prevent wind erosion. The bottom of these pits is usually levelled and any excess material is

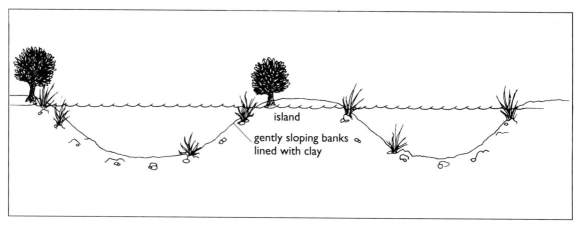

Modern, landscaped gravel pit. Not many features.

island
gently sloping banks lined with clay

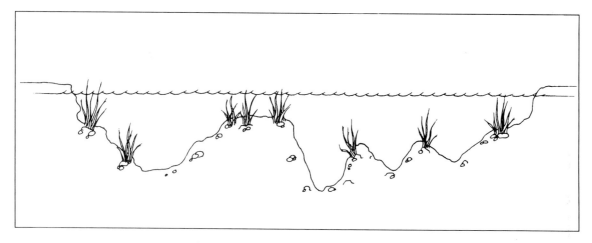

Older type pit with spoils dumped in bottom. Plenty of interesting features.

usually formed into islands. They look a little clinical to start with but will be the basis for some excellent fisheries in the future.

How do these factors affect the pike fishing? The old pits with numerous features are probably more interesting to fish as there will be well-defined routes that pike will travel and places where they are likely to be encountered. Channels between bars are an obvious place as are deeper weedy corners. On the newer-type pit with the even bottom, pike can often be caught by using sit-and-wait tactics because they roam far and wide over the plain expanse of even water and will eventually find your bait. Positioning of baits does not seem to be so critical here.

In order to catch more than just the lucky few pike you will need a good knowledge of the bottom contours. Plumbing is time-consuming and limited, especially on large or weedy pits. It is best to get a boat on the water and better still to make use of an electronic depth-finder. You will be surprised what you find. In many cases, the deeper water is close in and the best swims might not necessarily involve casting to the horizon. Try to locate the deepest hole from which the water will have been pumped during excavation. It is nearly always close to the bank and often adjacent to a waterway into which excess water has been pumped. This can be a useful cold-weather swim. In addition, seeing the reality of the weed in some of these pits from a boat will change your ideas on bait presentation completely. Many are simply underwater jungles!

Unknown Quantities

Having described typical pits that one might encounter, what can you expect when you enter the unknown and fish a water that you know nothing about. Keep an open mind until you are sure of your facts. In my routine exploration of pits, I fished one after following up a lead from a pleasure angler who had been getting tench mauled by pike as he reeled them in. After a couple of sessions I wrote it off. Within the limitations of the knowledge that I then had, the pit looked too new and barren to hold big pike. My instinctive feeling was that I did not fancy it at all.

Over the next three seasons, a chain of events led me to fish there again and take six thirty-pounders, four of which were different fish.

Until you start catching pike and getting recaptures you will never know the true picture of what is in there. If you do not catch any big pike at all, it is very frustrating to decide whether to carry on with it. You need to be a little philosophical about these things and enjoy the fact that you are at least doing a bit of pioneering. Fishing easier, more productive waters in between helps alleviate any despondency. I do not mind admitting that I often do a bit of reading or enjoy listening to the radio when sitting it out on these 'heart-break' waters. Above all, I enjoy the challenge as I have now got the confidence to know that every now and again, it pays dividends.

Waters with huge pike are, as I have found, the exception rather than the rule. Pike find their way into most pits very early on and seem to do very well if left alone but that happens very rarely.

TACKLING PITS

Let us look at tackle and tactics for these pits. Choice of rods is a difficult one because theoretically you need many different ones to cope with the many situations that will present themselves. Much of the fishing that I do is at quite close range and 12-foot, $2\frac{1}{4}$lb test curve, through-action rods are more than adequate. Then again, some of my 'under-the-rod' tactics involve dropping baits close to sunken branches and heavy weedbeds and a 3lb test curve through-action rod is necessary to haul them out. The 3lb test curve rods are also used for drifting baits at long range so that I can make early contact with a fish and keep the hooks in, not to mention their use for casting bigger baits like full herrings out a very long way. I do not enjoy playing pike on such stiff, hefty rods but they are necessary to do the job properly. Then there are all the situations 6in between where my 12-foot, $2\frac{1}{2}$lb test-curve, through-action rods are most suitable. They are adequate for most of my medium-range fishing and are very nice to play fish on. I am fortunate

That looks tasty.

to have rods to suit all situations because I am involved in the tackle trade but if I had to give them all back except one pair, they would be the MB2 2½ lb test curve, Waterwolf rods which will deal perfectly with all but the extremes of piking.

My Shimano reels and high-abrasion-resistant lines, mentioned elsewhere, will cater for all my pit piking needs. Of course, I will be lure fishing too, especially in October, and my lure tackle will generally be taken with me until it gets bitterly cold and the pike will not respond.

Pit piking has often been described as casting a deadbait to the horizon and waiting. Very often that is all you do and I do not intend to make it sound a lot more complicated than it really is. Luckily most of the pike that I fish for are not too far out and can be reached without employing specialized distance tactics. In fact, all of my thirties have come within 70 yards range and most of

them were taken a lot closer. Only in cases of severe angling pressure have I found it necessary to cast any further.

As I enjoy watching a float, I usually use this approach in my deadbaiting. I do this for fun and no other reason! I always use non-self-cocking floats and pull the line tight after casting so that they settle at a slight angle. This is vitally important if deep hooking is to be avoided. Self-cocking floats, which seem to be popular with a lot of anglers, can travel a long way without going under or showing a positive run, especially when a pike is moving slowly with the bait. An angler needs to be very observant with these floats, particularly when fished well overdepth. With the non-cocking float, set to the correct depth, and clipped up tight at the rod, the float either stands up and slowly goes under or sometimes lays flat if the pike rises in the water with the bait. This

Inserting polystyrene to a deadbait to give buoyancy.

cannot happen with the self-cocking float and it will only go under on a fast run.

Depth setting is important when float fishing deadbaits to ensure quick run-indication. I have noticed that a lot of anglers set them too far overdepth and this delays indication. For quick positive indication I like to set the float about 18 inches overdepth for bottom-fished baits and about 2½ feet overdepth with buoyant baits to reduce the risk of bite-offs. Incidentally, when I cast a deadbait rig out into a weedy pit I gently take in a couple of feet of line as the rig sinks so that everything goes down to the bottom in a straight line. This reduces the chances of the trace catching on the main line should it catch weed on the way down. This could again lead to a bite-off. Particular care is needed in this respect with buoyant baits which naturally 'hang' in the water on the way down.

Another thing that I like about floats is that they keep you constantly informed regarding the positions of your baits. When legering it is often difficult to remember precisely where you have cast a bait. With a float, it is easier to judge where to recast to next depending upon whether you want to get back into the same position or cast somewhere else. Floats tell you other things too. By lining them up with far bank features you can tell if they have moved and, very often, if you are observant, you will note that pike pick up baits and quickly drop them. There might not be much that you can do about it but it can give confidence in knowing that there is a pike in the swim or give you a chance to ask yourself why this should happen.

I have found that it is important in pit fishing, as with deadbaiting in many circumstances, to move the bait occasionally to attempt to induce a take or alternatively to fish it in a new position where it is more likely to be taken. With a very uneven bottom it is so easy for the bait to be just off patrol route and in a place where, for whatever reason, pike do not go. Attempting to move legered baits simply ends up with snagging in weed. A float-fished bait with just a few swan shot on the trace can be easily moved and its new position noted should you get a take and wish to recast there.

I choose to leger only when I wish to fish beyond the range of my floats which is about 65 yards on a normal day and 80 yards with a good wind behind me. It gets difficult to see them anyway at this range in certain light conditions. Where I am legering in weed, I do not really like to use 2½oz to 3oz leads, but sometimes this is the only way to get the range required. If I do have to do this I use a bait that will definitely be inside a good pike's mouth as soon as it moves away, and a rig which gives positive indication at the rod. This means using smallish baits of about six inches and preferably soft ones that will not be so easily levered out when the pike shakes its head. My preference is for a fresh smelt or sardine. With a bigger bait it would be tempting to wait just a little longer before striking and risk an angle being created between the fish and the angler via the heavy lead. This would reduce the striking efficiency at such range and fish are more likely to drop off in the long haul to get them back to the bank. For legering baits, especially where long waits are expected, there is nothing to beat the backbiter type indicator.

Long-Range Tactics

There are many long-range leger rigs for piking in the pits. Having tried quite a few I prefer the one that incorporates a hollow lead fixed to a length of semi-rigid rig tube with the bait to it with P.V.A. string. The tubing must be six inches longer than the trace and it should incorporate a small ring whipped to it for tying the P.V.A. to, which prevents it from sliding. On the cast, the lead leads the bait and with a semi-frozen bait, the whole lot flies out like a rocket. The P.V.A. takes about 30 seconds to dissolve in water at 5°C but is a lot quicker at higher temperatures. After a while, I draw the rig towards me slightly to ensure that the trace is not lying on the tube, risking a bite-off. The likelihood of this happening is small and I have never had one yet because I always take this precaution and use 'bite-proof' tubing. I still do this with a buoyant bait which, in theory, should rise in the water but it might be trapped underneath the tube. If I am not trying for extreme range, I do not bother with the P.V.A.

This sounds complicated but it is actually very simple and effective. Buoyant materials such as polystyrene or balsa can be used in the bait if it is tied to the trace. Alternatively, you can use a 20mm poly-ball tied to the trace which will lift the bait above the bottom debris. This is virtually identical to the livebait rig I describe in the section on Fen drain fishing and it is very easy to change from livebait to deadbait.

Livebaits Versus Deadbaits

Whether to use livebaits or deadbaits is a question that confronts every piker. If given a choice I would try both, but much of the pit fishing that I do virtually eliminates the possibility of livebaiting effectively. Drifted baits rarely get very far before finding weed to catch on. In order to place baits a good distance over uneven and weedy terrain, one must set them very shallow to allow for the worst conditions. In October, this might work quite well but as the water gets colder and colder, the pike are less likely to rise so far for a bait and results are not nearly so good. Paternostering works well if you know exactly where the weed-free patches are in which to place the baits. The only alternative is to use long paternoster links, which cause snagging up and a lot of frustration. The frustration is so severe in the weedy pits that I fish, that livebaiting is only carried out where I know I will get runs reasonably quickly or where nothing else will work. During October, for example, it is likely that small fish will be starting to shoal in some corners of pits, and shallow-fished roaming livebaits are very effective and easy to fish. On the trout-stocked pits that I fish, deadbaits produce virtually nothing but the odd jack or trout and I have to use livebait or I catch nothing. As an experiment on these waters I have actually left deadbaits out on cotton lines and markers for days on end and they have remained untouched apart from the rainbows moving them around.

Livebaiting can be very frustrating but fortunately deadbaiting is so devastating at times that I do not worry too much. I know that at times livebaits would be an advantage but there is no point worrying about it if I cannot fish them properly. There is no point in frustrating myself with the continual snagging up.

Deadbaiting is not a lazy option. To make it work to its best advantage there are a few things to consider. Obviously the bait must be rigged correctly to overcome weed and the pike's wariness but it must also be cast to where the pike are. In most pits, there are seasonal areas that are better than others. In order to discover where the pike are I believe in doing exactly what I do on any other water. Mobility is important. Where banks are easy to tread this might involve leap-frogging the rods, much as one would do on a Fenland drain. Where banks are difficult or swims are well-defined this might mean moving the tackle wholesale to a new area. Rod-pods are very useful on gravel pits where rests cannot be

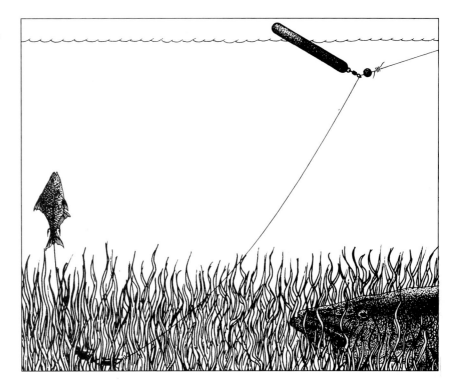

Making deadbaits more effective in weedy water by popping them up with buoyant material.

Rod-pods are ideal where the banks are too hard for rod-rests such as gravel pits and reservoir dams.

Rod-pods also make moving swim very easy.

pushed easily into hard banks. When moving swim, which is frequently necessary, it is so easy to pick up the pod, complete with rods and indicators, and move on.

Often, this mobile approach suddenly transformed a bad day as I have dropped onto some good fish. This is not something that falls into place in a few hours and it often pays to make several visits to a water and try many different areas before drawing conclusions or giving up too easily. Naturally from season to season you will be able to make judgements more quickly by getting to know a water. This being done, there is often then a case for sticking it out longer in swims that have proven themselves in the past.

Recently, I have had difficulty in getting to the water for daybreak. I am very aware, especially in

October, that I could have missed an important feeding time and I am probably fishing for pike that are not particularly active. They are likely to be lying quietly somewhere digesting a meal. If I can drop a bait on their noses I might be in with a chance. With this in mind I usually give a swim only an hour and a half or so and then cast to a new area or move swims. This has worked so many times that I do it with great confidence.

AN OCTOBER THIRTY

I remember well one occasion when mobile tactics put me onto a very big pike. I had just nipped over the fence of a derelict gravel working for a short session. There were two good swims on the bank that I had chosen to tackle and, with four hours ahead of me, I had decided to spend a couple of hours or so in each and see how things went. The early October day was idyllic with only a light ripple and warm, bright sunshine. At this time of year, the pike were as likely to be in the shallow water as in the deeper water so I decided to fish both over the session.

At first I opted for the shallows. These consisted of rows and rows of visible bars with holes, five or six feet deep, in between them. The whole area was thick with bottom weed. Buoyant deadbaits were cast as far as possible and pulled back to drop into deeper water. The amount of swan shot used on the trace was only just enough to sink the bait to minimize the risk of snagging up. Every half an hour the baits were inched back and I attempted to drop them into the next visible

trough. I was not too bothered if the ba the shallow water near the top of because, in the warm October sunshine, just as likely a place to get a run as in the s. deeper holes.

After a couple of hours of moving baits recasting to new areas, I was not entirely su prised that I had not had a run. It was that type of water! There were very few pike but there were a couple of very big ones amongst them. However, these never gave themselves up easily as they were very well-fed. Just as I was thinking about moving to the other swim, the gravel company foreman appeared on the bank a few hundred yards away and not too far from where I wanted to fish next. He was discussing the clearance of an adjacent ditch with an excavator driver and I was hoping that he would leave so that I

Setting up for a long wait with the E.T. double backbiter alarm.

could fish! If he had seen me I would have been asked to go without a doubt as he only ever allowed a few close friends to fish there. Time was ticking away and I was getting increasingly frustrated. He just would not leave. There were plenty of bushes and tall grasses between us, so I decided to take a chance. Piece by piece, my equipment was ferried into position with me, at times, on hands and knees so as not to be seen. Once down the steep bank, I took a chance and cast to the deep water. Out into the ten-foot deep swim went my three favourite buoyant deadbaits: a herring, a smelt and a trout. As each one plopped into the swim, I just kept still and waited for a few minutes before tightening up and putting the line in an elastic band on the rod butt. Rod-rests were dispensed with and I sat with three rods at my feet, half in and half out of the water. Luckily, a light breeze sprung up, otherwise my three orange-tipped floats would have stood out like beacons.

This was a lovely place to fish and only a few really keen local pikers knew of its potential. The water was absolutely gin clear and the bottom weed luxurious. Occasionally, quality rudd and tench could be seen patrolling the margins and any pike feeding on these had to grow rapidly in a rich water only twelve years old. I seem to get mesmerized by my floats when I fish in this way and continually scan them, imagining what it will look like when a bait gets taken. After only five minutes in the swim, the buoyant trout was taken. The stick float stood up straight, gave four or five very violent jabs and shot away. As I looked down, the line had tightened to the elastic band and I released it to allow line to run out. It was absolutely belting out and after about fifteen seconds I wound down fast towards the fish and swept the rod upwards giving two firm but gentle digs to be sure of a good hook-hold. I never released the pressure or gave slack line. For the first 30 seconds of a fight, I never give any slack line at all as sometimes the pike will just be gripping a bait tightly. If it lets go and the line is tight there is a good chance that the hooks will catch but on a slack line it could blow it away.

After seven or eight minutes of gaining line by inches, the fish obviously was not coming off and it was a very heavy powerful pike. When it decided to power away or change direction I could do little about it and had to go with it. All the time, in the distance, I could hear the foreman and the ditch-digger talking and I imagined being caught and made to return the fish without weighing it!

Trying to keep the rod low I inched the pike closer. I would have preferred to keep the rod up with a good bend in it but had little choice in case it was seen. Finally she came up on top, thrashed the surface and then headed down towards the work men. The water heaved and boiled and occasionally the fish broke the silence as she surfaced. Surely they could hear it and see the disturbance coming from the swim. However, they did not and inch by inch she came to the net. The only way to net a really heavy fish on your own is to let her come very slowly to the net while you and the net remain perfectly still. With no hooks showing she went over the draw string and, as happens with many big fish, I could not quite lift the net to get the last inch or so of her massive frame over the drawstring so I dropped the rod to use both hands and make sure. At last she was in!

After sitting quietly for a minute or two, savouring the sight of a massive mottled back lying there in the midday sun, I formulated a plan to finish the job properly. The fish was made safe in an E.T. mega-sack then, on hands and knees, so as to remain unseen, I painstakingly packed all the tackle away. All that was left out was the weighing gear and the photographic equipment. The tripod and camera were made ready in a little clearing behind some bushes and out of sight. The huge fish was hauled up the bank and quickly weighed. The 44-inch fish weighed 30lb 3oz! Two quick shots were taken off each side and she was carried back in the sack to the water's edge. I really enjoyed this as I knew I had got away with it. I did not really care if I was caught now as I sat for a few minutes and held her great tail until she was ready to go. As it happened, they did not catch me and I slipped away quietly, unnoticed, with another adventure to tell over dinner back home.

April: A 23½lb pike, only 37in long, taken from a trout fishery and destined for restocking in another water.

April: A 26lb 6oz pike, 44in long, taken from a trout reservoir on retrieved deadbait tactics. Best of a catch of 7 doubles totalling 125lb.

*: A pike as big as a boy! Young Daniel shares the glory of catching a 28lb 1oz pike,
long, taken from a trout reservoir on drifted perch livebait.*

*May: 20lb 11oz pike taken from an Irish Lough on
long-range legered goat fish deadbait.*

*June: 27lb 13oz pike, 41in long, taken from a trout
reservoir on drifted roach livebait. This fish took fifteen
minutes to land.*

June: The 'Gailey monster', which bottomed the scales
out at 32lb 12oz. This 43in fish, taken in late June,
took a drifted perch livebait.

July: 19lb 10oz pike taken from a Severn weirpool
on a 40g red-head pattern, Abu Hi-Lo.

July: 21lb 4oz pike taken just after dark on a crucian livebait from a small Midlands water.

September: Three big doubles taken in quick succession from the Severn on trotted livebaits near a large sunken tree.

August: My personal best lure-caught pike, weighing 28lb 12oz, taken from a Lincolnshire pit on a sinking Rapala lure.

August: A beautifully marked thirteen-pounder from a Lincolnshire pit, taken on a Lindy tandem blade spinner-bait.

November: 26lb pike from Bough Beech reservoir on a paternostered live trout in over 20ft of water.

November: 23lb 5oz drain pike taken under the rod tip on a large roach livebait.

December: 22lb Broadland pike taken on a float-fished buoyant herring from the Thurne system.

December: 30lb 10oz gravel-pit pike taken at close range on a dead perch.

problems to solve. Most of these waters are massive with their acreages in the hundreds. Location becomes a problem on a grand scale. There are two approaches that you can take if you fish these waters. The commonest one seems to be to see where the fish are coming from and move into that area! This might bring short-term success but will not benefit you if you wish improve your pike fishing skills. As this is a practice that really annoys people, I will do no more than mention it in passing.

The alternative is to make use of the modern high-tech equipment that can help you to more quickly understand the nature of these waters and assess where the pike may be. For me, to fish from a boat on a big water is a chance to develop these unfamiliar skills. Boat fishing on rivers, pits and broads is one thing, but this is boat fishing of a very different nature.

As the waters are bigger, then so too must be the boats in order for them to be safe to use there. Rowing is usually out and motors, either petrol or electric, are used. Apart from taking too long to row around these huge waters, it would be almost impossible when the wind really starts to make the water roll. Some fisheries provide petrol engines and others allow you to take your own engine. This is sometimes restricted to the use of electric only. Modern types like the Shakespeare and Minn Kota are marvellous and so quiet and efficient, they are a pleasure to use. They require a special battery known as a deep-cycle cell which requires a special charger. A fully charged, heavy-duty battery lasts several days if you use it sensibly. If you use a hired petrol motor, make sure you listen to the instructions for working it, otherwise you could find yourself stuck waiting for assistance and wasting good

Seagull petrol motor and fuel can. Shakespeare electric trolling motor, battery and charger.

fishing time. Even if you are not too used to boats, it should not take long to get the hang of things. Most event organizers will insist on you using a life jacket and not to do so is foolish, especially when the water is icy cold and a heavy wind is blowing.

The next important piece of equipment you will need is a depth finder or fish locator. Simple depth locators, useful as they are, now seem to be almost totally superseded by fish locators. It is often said that using fish locators is cheating. On a three-acre pond I would agree but on reservoirs of hundreds of acres it is sensible to use technology to enable you to do certain jobs a lot more quickly. Life would not be long enough to fish even a handful of these waters successfully without the benefits that locators provide. Apart from showing fish, their other prime function is to scan the depth and bottom contours. This information can be displayed on a screen that changes as new

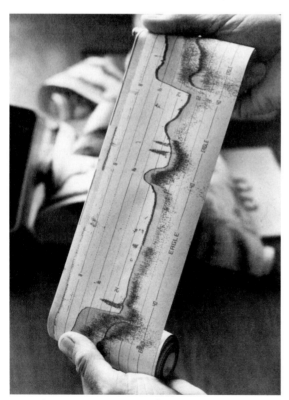

Studying the underwater details from a chart made with a Lowrance computer graph recorder.

terrain is passed over or, on some machines, it can even be permanently recorded on a printed chart. After an hour with such a piece of equipment, your outlook is transformed forever as you realize that you are crossing over bars, troughs, sunken forests and even derelict buildings. With this information as a guide you can now decide how to tackle the depths beneath you and set the tackle accurately to suit. That is the theory, but believe me, the fish do not suddenly start climbing your rods, even with this invaluable knowledge!

When using the fish-finder function, you will be staggered to learn that there are vast areas without any fish at all. On a 7,000-acre water, I have motored for three miles without picking up a fish signal! At other times I have gone over shoals of fish hundreds of yards long. Finding these shoals is no guarantee of success. I have usually been disappointed after dropping a bait into them. Getting to grips with this style of fishing is a very long-term exercise.

THE PIKE IN NOVEMBER

When bitter weather arrives, it may seem cold to us because we are warm-blooded creatures, but the pike's body temperature varies with water temperature. It may well notice and be affected by sudden changes in temperature but once temperatures stabilize, no matter how cold, they adjust and feed according to their needs. Just as our common sense or instinct tells us to wrap up warmly and take plenty of food and warm drinks in this cold weather, the pike's instinct tells it to keep its belly full to be able to cope with the difficult times ahead. Herein lies a possible reason why some waters are better than others when it gets colder. Where pike are well-fed, they will lie contented at low temperatures whereas if they are not so lucky, they may have to keep looking for food for longer and that gives us more opportunity to catch them. So never forget that if you are out piking in November, the pike are probably out there feeding somewhere no matter how inhospitably the day dawns. Sudden temperature drops do reduce sport though sudden increases

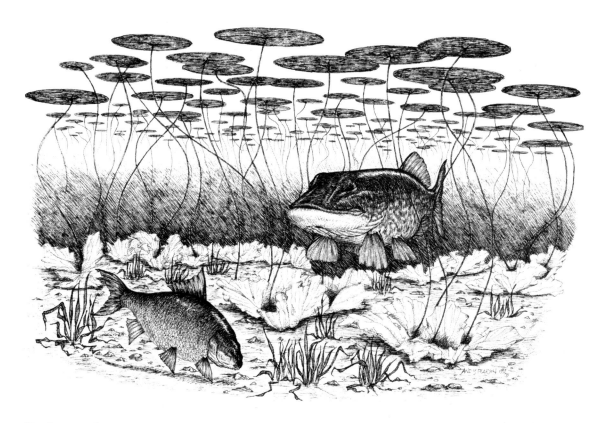

Death approaches.

may improve it. However, it is going to get a lot colder yet!

A POSITIVE APPROACH

It is actually quite rare in this month for the temperature to drop to such an extent that sport is killed off for very long. It is more likely that a very cold night which produces a picturesque frost will be followed by a still, sunny day with all signs of the frost gone by ten o'clock. I have had many gruelling starts only to find out that by this hour I have needed to peel my jumper off. This reminds me of a little advice that I keep giving myself in times of low morale whenever I am faced with a grim weather forecast. Never be put off by forecasts of doom and gloom by either the weatherman or other anglers. It is so easy to take

a negative approach and decide that it will be a waste of time going out and that you are unlikely to catch much. I have stayed in bed several times thinking like this, only to realize by mid-morning that I have made a big mistake because the weather has improved. Be an optimist and you will not miss as much action. However, you will have an awful day every now and again, but you can always go home or do what I tend to do on days of extreme weather conditions.

Days when there are heavy frosts or snow falls or times when rivers are in flood are ideal for getting unusual and spectacular photographs simply of landscapes or of anglers fishing. Many pike anglers enjoy capturing the atmosphere of their hobby on film, and these are often times to get some really good material. You can also make that extra bit of effort and look at places that you always intended to look at but never got round to.

Piking is not just about going through the motions of fishing but also doing this ground work and gathering information.

DRAIN PIKE

In this chapter I look at tactics for the Fen Drains as this is the time of year I like to make a more determined start on them. Most of my observations have been made on the drains in my own locality in the east of England but having fished in drains in Somerset and in Holland, I think my comments are equally valid for most of these man-made waters. Compared to the beauty of such places as the Wye Valley or the Norfolk Broads one could be forgiven for describing the Fens as boring, uninteresting and featureless. That is the sort of remark that I get from visiting anglers who fish the drains with me.

They are right of course, at least in part, for the beauty and interest in the Fen fishing is a hidden one. The visitor tends to only see the popular well-trodden places that are near to the roads and bridges. The fishing there is, at best, only mediocre. Here and there, though, are out of the way places, at the ends of rarely-travelled tracks, where surprises abound. In the waterlogged marshland areas where man rarely goes, you are likely to see almost every water bird that you can think of, including the very rare bittern. At dawn and dusk you will be inspected by several different species of owl and hares and rabbits pop up at any time. It is not always windy and raining either, even though it may seem so at times. Many a wild day drifts into an incredible sunset, exaggerated by the flat horizon and massive skyscape. They say beauty is in the eye of the beholder and maybe this is a classic case.

What of the drain pike though? I should not really give this away, but the Fen piking is as good as I have ever known it. In the early seventies, when I started to be serious about my piking, the Fens were the mecca of pike anglers. The Broads had faded into obscurity and the potential of the trout reservoirs was yet to be realized. The Fens was the place where serious pikers headed after

following regular newspaper reports of big pike and zander catches to local pikers like Barrie Rickards, Neville Fickling and Bill Chillingsworth, to mention but a few. Without the Fens, anglers like myself and John Watson from Norwich, might not have got our piking off the ground in such a big way as we lived, at the time, in such poor piking areas. The Fens were a part of our awakening to what piking could offer.

The piking was first class then and is just as good now in many places although one or two waters are still in the doldrums due to the introduction of zander and actions of the Water Authority. Where it is not so good, it is largely because zander have taken over as the predominant predator. As I enjoy catching both species that causes me no problems.

The actual catching of drain pike is rarely difficult. The only problem as I see it is locating them. I hate to use this well-worn cliché but it sums it up very aptly. The fish are not evenly distributed like currants in a cake. There can be very long sections of drain which are totally devoid of pike and other short sections where they are packed tightly, particularly in wintertime. Sometimes these areas, once found, can be relied upon time and time again to produce pike and only excessive angling pressure will push them out. At other times, you can discover a lot of pike in a swim and never find them there again. Without local knowledge, the visiting angler will have to work hard to find pike and keep in touch with them. Finding them initially can be a problem but there are one or two things that can reduce the odds to some extent.

The Fenlands are criss-crossed with hundreds of drains of all sizes. Most have pike in and many could turn up twenty-pounders. The small side drains often hold pike too, but some are susceptible to low water problems and pollution from farm chemicals. Most of the main drains can be fished on either day-tickets or cheap club cards. A good start is to gather information from whoever is selling the tickets. The next rule of thumb is that swims close to access points have usually been fished heavily by anglers who cannot be bothered to walk any further and whilst these can

Fen drain piking has its distractions like this 10lb 11oz zander from a once prolific pike water.

turn up the occasional big pike, this is not a reliable way to start. I would always walk well away from the access point before the start of fishing.

Until you find some fish, you have a lot of work ahead of you. The essence of drain fishing is to keep moving until you find the fish. The practice of leap-frogging the rods, that is working along the water by occasionally moving the trailing rod in front of the leading rod, appears to have originated in the Fens or at least is well associated with drain fishing and it is an important technique to make use of. It works too. I have many times covered hundreds of yards of water to no avail only to find that a move to a fresh swim has produced several runs immediately or even a big haul. As often as not you do not drop on a large concentration of pike but you can still pick up plenty of fish while moving from swim to swim.

This does not often happen if you sit in the same spot all day and wait for them to come to you.

This is only a simplistic view of locating pike. Other factors must be taken into account. For example, feeding times are important. If the hot feeding time is at dawn, and you do not reach the swim where they are until mid-day, then you have missed your chance and might only tempt the odd fish or two. Furthermore, the pike may have a feeding preference. If this is for livebaits and you are only using deadbaits, you might only scratch the surface of the potential of the swim. These preferences certainly exist. In not all cases, but many, I have noted that this preference for livebaits occurs amongst congregations of prey fish. Of course, the prey fish do not always give away their presence, so if you do not use both approaches you will never know.

Mick Rouse playing a lively pike on a remote Fenland drain.

Only recently I experienced a good example of this. I was catching roach for bait on a local drain and fished a deadbait on a second rod to add a little interest. I fished all day and caught dozens of baits. The deadbait produced one run all day. The children were with me and just to keep them occupied I gave them a rod which I set up to make use of the very small roach that I did not want to use as baits myself. With no knowledge of pike fishing whatsoever they caught six pike to 10lb 5oz with the biggest going to Nicola, aged nine! A five-hour session on my own in that swim later produced twenty-two pike for a total of well over 100lb and all to livebaits! Never ignore these preferences, not only on drains, but on all waters.

Unless you know exactly where the fish are, the key to drain piking is mobility. This means travelling light and keeping the tackle weight and the bulk to a minimum. I tend to do this anyway, as

a matter of course, and umbrellas, bivvies and holdhalls are rarely a part of my equipment. If you are travelling some distance to fish the Fen drains your approach will probably by very different from that of a local angler. A visitor will spend a large proportion of his time searching for areas with good numbers of pike whilst a local angler, knowing these locations, will spend his time moving from one to another and the latter naturally has a distinct advantage. Fortunately, the searching process is made less painful because in general on the Fens the banks are flat and even and easy to negotiate. Considering that you might cover the best part of a mile in a day's fishing this helps a great deal.

I would like to look at this searching process through the eyes of someone who is new to Fenland. As with any pike fishing, you would be wise to gather any information beforehand regarding

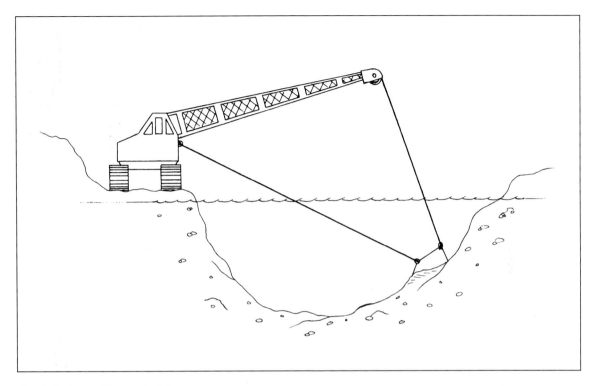

Plumb drains carefully as dredging contours can vary.

likely venues. Just taking a chance and fishing at the first drain that you come to is too hit and miss. If you keep an eye on match results and in particular the results of pike matches on the Fens, you will get some good indications of where to fish and often where not to fish. I cringe sometimes, when these results are printed, and some of my favourite places are mentioned! Keep an eye on locations where the regular good match weights are coming from. As the winter progresses it will often be noted that certain pegs always produce the winning catches as roach and bream shoal tightly. A lot of these venues are permanently pegged and the peg numbers are often referred to and easy to find.

When the weather gets colder and prey fish shoal tightly on the drains, they often give themselves away by dimpling the surface. Where there are huge concentrations, there are often an incredible number of pike with them. When this happens the pike give themselves away by chasing fish to the surface occasionally. These are

exceptional cases though and most areas with plenty of prey fish and hence pike are not so easily found. One way of spotting pike is to be on the drain at the crack of dawn and, if you are lucky, prey fish will be seen dimpling for a short while. They usually do not show again until dusk, so if you arrive in the middle of the day you could miss this encouraging sign.

A practice that I would suggest to a group of anglers exploring a huge drain system for the first time is to spread out and fish as many places as possible. Gather information regarding potential places beforehand and arrange for each person to fish a different one. Meet up at the end of the day and exchange details of findings. In this way things will fall into place more quickly.

The actual fishing when exploring a section of drain can change from being very boring to being hectic within a very short time. It is possible to cover hundreds of yards without a run and then, by dropping onto an accumulation of pike, have two or three runs simultaneously. How often to move is a problem and I have a rule of thumb which I apply. The smaller the drain, the faster I move along it. A swim on a small drain, perhaps only 15 to 20 yards wide, can be fished out very quickly if you go about it correctly. At the other extreme, a swim on a very big drain of over 80 yards wide could take hours to cover properly. Then there are the intermediate sizes. It is a matter of putting a selection of baits into the most likely positions and giving the pike time to inspect and take them. In drains of all sizes this has to include the near bank shelf, and some of the biggest drain pike and zander I have caught have come from right under the rod tip. This being the case, it is essential to be very quiet on the bank but it is amazing how many anglers do not seem to realize or take heed of this. This might be why I catch far more fish when alone because I do everything quietly and carefully.

The far bank shelf is just as important, but the wider the drain, the more difficult it is to fish it efficiently. Sometimes the bait has to be absolutely tight to this feature to get a take. Sometimes these features may have something to enhance them like weed beds, overhanging bushes or remains of submerged cabbage patches but as often as not they do not. Although these are prime places to position baits, never neglect the open water which turns up plenty of fish on some days, especially when the water has a little colour.

On small to medium-sized drains I have a standard practice that ensures that I cover the water well and which catches me plenty of pike. Until I find pike, I prefer to concentrate mainly on livebaiting which I feel will be the method that will succeed when the going is difficult. Until you start to catch you must assume that it will be difficult. Being mobile means doing a lot of casting and to do it properly you need plenty of bait. Twenty to thirty good baits will suffice for a full day and you should have some good baits for freezing afterwards. As casting is the thing that kills baits quickly (apart from pike that is!) I like to fish a livebait under the near bank which can normally be just lowered into position. On the far bank ledge I put a deadbait. If I am expecting pike I prefer a fresh smelt or roach. Any sea or freshwater fish, including eel section, will

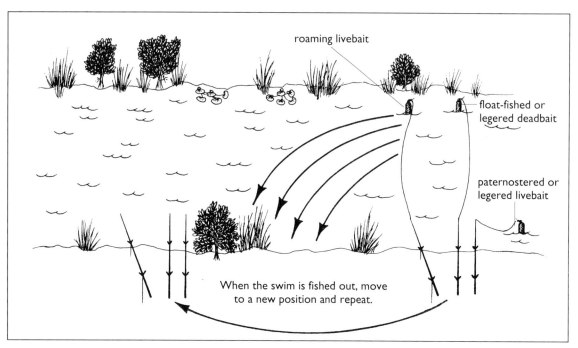

roaming livebait

float-fished or legered deadbait

paternostered or legered livebait

When the swim is fished out, move to a new position and repeat.

An approach for systematically fishing a small drain.

normally do provided that it is fresh and of a decent size, say six or seven inches. With the added possibility of some big zander, I might use coarse fish exclusively to improve my chances of getting them too. Zander have a distinct preference for coarse fish and eels and they rarely take sea fish baits.

Where possible I like to use a float for indication but this is not always possible due to heavy winds and drifting weed. On a flat calm day I might use an orange-tipped stick float for deadbaiting and a carefully set surface float paternoster at the near bank. The reason, as I have mentioned elsewhere is simply because I like to watch the floats going under. More practically however, especially in rough weather, I use different tactics and usually leger both the live and deadbaits and clip the lines up tight at the rod. If I am moving very fast, as on a very small drain, I will use a simple drop-off sight bobbin. On a larger drain where I will spend much longer in a swim I will use a backbiter alarm. The leger rig I use has changed over recent years. Initially I used a standard set-up where the bait settled on the

bottom. Many anglers on the drains, myself included, have seen the advantage of the off-bottom rig, originally designed for catfish, that incorporates a small polyball on the trace. This has the benefit of keeping deadbaits above the bottom debris or thick slimy mud and keeps livebaits working actively.

Back to the fishing. The two static rigs, one deadbait and one livebait, need little attention for a while, although I continually keep an eye on the indicators. This leaves me free to put a third rod to use and search a lot of water using a suitable technique. There are three techniques that I use on my 'searching rod' and the one I employ depends upon water conditions and bait availability. This is carried out, incidentally, in the strip of water adjacent to the other baits, and I position myself no more than a few yards away from these rods. I also attempt to remain quiet and concealed.

My favourite approach, if I have plenty of bait, is to drift livebaits through the swim. The bait is set up on a normal greased-line roaming-livebait rig and cast to the far bank. In November I would

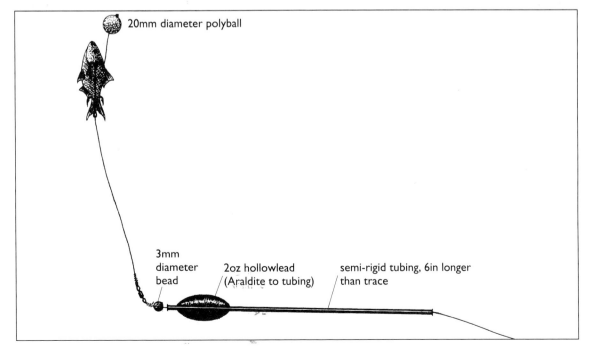

20mm diameter polyball

3mm diameter bead

2oz hollowlead (Araldite to tubing)

semi-rigid tubing, 6in longer than trace

Off-bottom leger rig for live- or deadbaiting.

set it to be just off-bottom and allow the wind to take it down the drain as far as possible until it came into the near bank. Takes can come anywhere but very often they come against the near bank. About six drifts round usually kills the bait or makes it ineffective so the number of times that you can do this is limited.

If livebaits are in short supply, do not worry too much because the dead fish can then be rigged on a simple wobbled bait set-up and very slowly inched back as close to the bottom as possible. Some days, when the pike are especially active, this rod will get plenty of takes and I reel in the other baits and work down the drain with just this one rod.

I always have my lures to fall back on. At one time this was considered a last resort but I am just starting to appreciate how effective lures can be in these situations. I usually take lures with me to suit the depth of water to be fished, taking into consideration the colour of the water and the fact that they will probably have to be worked quite slowly. Dutch anglers I have spoken to lure fish all through the winter with good results and maybe a lot more British anglers will progress in this direction once they gain confidence.

After a period of fishing a livebait and a deadbait and also working a mobile bait through the swim, the angler will know himself when it is time to try somewhere else. How far to move is always a problem and I am afraid that there is no easy answer. By skipping a section you could easily miss a stack of fish and by moving too slowly along the drain you might never come to them! As with any fishing, you will be lucky to be successful overnight and will have to put in a lot of

Weighing a big pike using an E.T. sling and Avon scales while afloat on a trout water. Note E.T. unhooking mat on floor of boat to protect fish when unhooking.

effort. This being the case, it is important to enjoy what you are doing and feel confident that you are fishing the swim effectively. Once you gain confidence and start catching, drain piking can be just as exciting as anywhere else.

9 DECEMBER – HARD DAYS, HARD MEN

EVIL WEATHER

December can be a very testing time. If I had any sense I would take December off and have a break from piking when the really cold weather arrived. Perhaps I would not have so many aches and pains now from sitting out in the past in boats and on banks, enduring evil, biting winds and icy cold water. In a real December, air temperatures can hover around zero, and water temperatures are not much higher. Pike activity slows right down, but rarely to a complete standstill. In numbing frosts or fierce gales coming in off the North Sea, the only pikers that will be about are the real hard men of the sport. Some might say that only the real 'nutters' would venture out in these conditions but this is not the case because to do so without proper preparation is asking for trouble. No, the people who do the job properly are not stupid and know a thing or two about what they are doing.

These anglers are out there with a purpose in mind which, as ever, is to catch pike. They know that it can so easily all come together despite the weather and enjoy the sense of achievement in beating adverse conditions. To stand there holding a huge, fat pike in frost-bitten hands is the target but, to them, success in any degree is creditable. This might be difficult for a casual observer to appreciate. The pike are there for the catching and with fewer anglers after them at this time, the chances of those seeking them increase.

The pike may be shoaled up tight. They might not be prepared to move too far and they might only feed for a very brief spell every now and again. They can be caught though and a tempting bait dropped in the right place at the right time might well produce a heart-stopping take, which is heightened by its unexpectedness. In milder conditions you usually expect to get plenty of takes but when they are few and far between, as in these conditions, they are appreciated so much more.

SURVIVAL

These pike anglers know something else too which is vital when setting forth to pike fish in these treacherous conditions. They know how to take care of themselves. No one is so tough that

Going to extremes to fish pike!

125

they can withstand hour after hour of cold and damp. Human beings are not made like that, except perhaps in fairy tales. Even the biggest and strongest amongst us will collapse if they allow their body temperature to drop too far. There are so many things that can befall the unprepared. What is the point in catching several big pike only to end up with hypothermia in the short term or arthritis later?

Preparation is important no matter what the piker does but now it is vital to survival. To survive, and at the same time successfully catch pike, is no easy task. The session ahead needs to be well thought-out and planned. Fishing in foul weather needs to be done with self-preservation as the first priority. I am not talking about a day on a local gravel pit where you fish a hundred yards from the car and if it gets cold you sit inside for a while and run the engine. That is kids' stuff! I am talking about setting out in a boat an hour before daylight to reach swims a good half hours motoring away and to fish till darkness falls again. I am talking bout walking a mile or two along a wild river valley to reach a remote spot, probably not seeing another living soul all day long and then trudging back in a blizzard. It may seem like madness but these are the things I want to do until the day I die. If something goes wrong in these conditions though, it can be fatal.

The first thing to do is to let someone know exactly where you are going and what time you will be back. At least if something does go wrong, you will know that someone will eventually find you. I once made the mistake of not doing this and was taken ill in the dark in a remote spot where I would not have been found for a very long time. Only careful preparation kept me alive as I lay unconscious on a freezing cold, January night. This might only happen once in a lifetime but why risk it? I usually leave a note on the kitchen table with a rough map of where I am, if I think that there is any real danger.

Clothing is the next priority and really today all you need is available. When I first started piking we had to make do with layer upon layer of trousers, jumpers and socks. We were still very cold! Nowadays, there is an incredible range of one-piece thermal suits, waterproofs and insulated footwear. My Bob Church one-piece wax cotton suit and thermal underwear will keep me warm and dry in any weather. I would never be without my wool scarf, thermal gloves and balaclava which make so much difference.

We can even bivvy out now with confidence, even when temperatures are so low that the water freezes over. The modern range of bed chairs, sleeping bags and accessories like stoves is tremendous and of a very high quality too. This is, indeed, a very good time to be entering the world of specialized angling.

Harsh weather has a way of bringing one very close to the natural elements which gives one a great deal of respect for them. On such sessions one can experience a real feeling of vulnerability. It can be quite disturbing if you push yourself too far and are too tired to row the boat against the wind or are too cold to walk any further. The realization that you could die is a sobering thought and has passed through my mind on many a December dusk, with a hard day behind me and a gruelling trek ahead of me along the slippery banks of a flooded, icy cold river.

Thank goodness at the end of such marathons there is the comfort of a modern motor vehicle. Most are, thankfully, very reliable if serviced correctly. Many are not though. A break-down on the motorway on the way to your auntie's is not the end of the world but to find yourself freezing cold on a remote track when the engine will not start could be. What do you do if this should happen? What if it rains heavily while you are fishing and you later find your wheels slipping and you cannot pull away? Generally, you will find a way out of it even if the last thing you want to do in the cold and dark is spend a couple of hours of frustrating physical exertion. Not getting into trouble in the first place and being prepared for anything is the answer. I now use a Nissan Patrol four-wheel drive, diesel vehicle for my fishing. Second-hand prices are quite reasonable and fuel consumption is not bad either. The diesel engine will go through floodwater without expiring and in four-wheel-drive I have been through mud axle-deep. Apart from this it is comfortable and

Cold – but happy!

roomy enough to carry all the gear that I will ever need and I can sleep in the back. It has a towing bar which enables me to pull heavy boats on trailers and has the gearing to slowly pull boats on trailers up steep ramps from the water. It is the perfect motor for a piker.

For extreme weather fishing, I always carry a couple of warm blankets in the vehicle, a Calor Gas stove and equipment for boiling water for a hot drink. On long trips to remote places, I even take a hot-water bottle with me when I am sleeping in the motor afterwards. Anyone who thinks that is funny has obviously never been out on a *really* gruelling session. It is strange how these situations bring home the fact that the things that give the most real pleasure are the basic requirements of food and warmth.

You may never have been in the kind of scrapes which would enable you to appreciate

what I am saying. In the last twenty-five years of piking, I have been in some awful situations. The more you fish, the more likely it is that something will eventually happen to you too, so do not ignore this warning. Always be prepared for the unexpected. I remember, for example, a time when I was fishing for livebait in the semi-darkness in the swim above the weir on the Severn at Tewkesbury. One minute I was lifting a dace to my hand and the next I was up to my waist in water and holding on for grim death as the bank collapsed beneath me. Luckily, John Sidley heard me calling and he hauled me out. With the lock-keeper's cottage only 200 yards away, I was soon drying out in front of a roaring fire and enjoying a warm meal. But what would have happened if I had been alone, and miles from anywhere? Even if I had got out of the icy cold water, would I have survived the cold?

Suitable clothing is essential for survival.

I was to find out on another lonely winter's night on the Severn. Netting a nineteen-pounder in the pitch black by the light of a small torch held in my teeth, the same thing happened again and I was soaked to the arm pits. The bank here was not too steep and I got out of the river quite easily. Elated as a result of catching such a nice fish I hung around to set up my tripod in order to get a photograph to remember the event. That was my big mistake, for the cold was creeping up on me yet, for a while, with the adrenalin flowing, I had not noticed. Suddenly I was shivering, my head was aching and I could hardly move my legs. Somehow I managed to get into the car, start the engine and turn the heater on full blast. I wrapped the two blankets I kept for emergency around me and I honestly wondered whether I had gone too far this time and whether I had finally netted my last pike. It was well over an hour before I had the strength to drive the fifty miles home.

Nowadays I always carry spare clothes and a towel on such trips. I was a much younger man at the time too and I wonder if I would get away with mistreating my body so badly now.

BACKWATER BONANZAS

I can feel a shiver coming over me as I remember some of those grim days of yesteryear – the characters I fished with and the adventures we had. Hopefully, many more are still to come. Sadly, some of those characters are no longer with us today. John Sidley was one of the most successful predator anglers that ever lived. John went as he would have wanted. On a gruelling day in wind and snow on his beloved River Severn, he

Returning a nineteen-pounder to a Severn backwater.

pushed himself too hard and paid the price. Rest in Peace, mate.

John and I were, I suppose, rivals in those days of long ago when we were both learning the ropes of pike fishing. Fate had taken us both, independently, to the Dead Arm of the River Severn at Tewkesbury in Gloucestershire. We were both looking for a change of venue when we stumbled upon piking which was nothing like either of us had experienced before. Aware of each other's reputations, we tried not to let each other know what we were catching, as we hoped to keep the water to ourselves. However, before too long, it was obvious that we had both discovered it. For

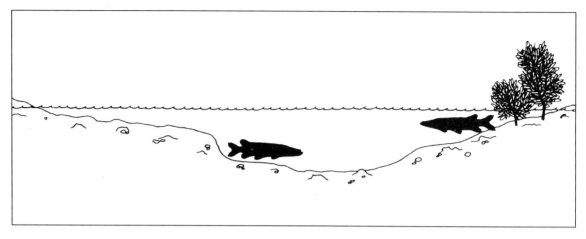

Typical cross-section of the Dead Arm.

the next three or four winters, we gave that back water everything and the pike catches were colossal with as many as nine doubles each in a session and many 100lb plus hauls. We would get to that water as if our lives depended upon it, always competing for the top swims; the tree, the barge and the cutting. The water nearly always produced something, no matter what the weather threw at us. Only extreme flood conditions or freezing over could ever have been classed as a waste of time. They were memorable days. I was so in love with fishing there that I used to sneak days off work just to get back to it. In bitterly cold weather, my boss would never have suspected that I had gone fishing! John became so obsessed with the water that he virtually lived there, spending many week-long sessions staying with Dave Jones, the lock-keeper. How I envied him!

The Arm is actually an old course of the river from the days before the weir and lock were built over a hundred years ago. It is now blocked at the upstream end but is still connected to the river via the lock cutting, which is used by boats to get around the weir. Naturally, the water level of the backwater rises and falls with that of the river. In a normal summer, there is hardly any water in there at all beyond the first couple of dozen yards. As the winter rains arrive, the river rises to its winter level and often higher still and it becomes a haven for all fish seeking refuge from the flow.

The water level starts this rise-and-fall procedure way back in October when the first noticeable rains arrive. The level goes up and down and fish move in and out with it. It is possible to catch a few pike at this time but never with any certainty. As flood follows flood and water temperatures start to drop rapidly, more and more pike and prey move in. By December they seem to be virtually resident in there especially if the river maintains a high level and a strong flow. As there are so many prey fish available and this is a prime spawning site for pike, abundant with sunken bushes and flooded grass, it is no wonder that they are drawn here from far and wide. This is the time when I like to start fishing there, not to mention the many other backwaters and sidestreams off the river. Most rivers have these places and where I live now in the east of England there are many good swims off the Welland and Nene, two local rivers.

Every backwater will be different and will need slightly different tactics. Most of the ones I have fished do not raise nearly as many problems as this one. After fishing here the others seem easy. The biggest problem is that this backwater is on a tidal river. Apart from the rise and fall of the river due to rainfall, the lower river is affected twice a day by tidal influences. This area is in fact the upstream limit of the major effect of the famous Severn Bore. Sometimes the tidal rise is but a few

The legendary 'Tree' swim on the Dead Arm of the Severn.

inches and is barely noticeable. At other times, it can rise by several feet and with alarming speed and has no respect for anything in its path. On one occasion the rise came in so fast that we had to abandon the rods! When high tides are due, I usually telephone the river information service and get details of heights and times. Because of this constant fluctuation in level, the banks are permanently caked in mud and silt. It really is the most messy place that I have ever fished! By the end of a typical day, a pair of Barbour over-trousers will stand up on their own!

With the river at normal winter level, most of the bank is fishable except for one area where the mud is exceptionally treacherous and cannot be trodden. Fishing is from one bank only and the opposite bank is lined with bushes and out of bounds. Initially I started to fish there in typical

fashion with a mixture of livebaits and sea and freshwater deadbaits. Very quickly a pattern emerged and livebaits outfished deadbaits to such an extent that deadbaiting was no longer considered. This was exactly what I found later in the main river itself. I was very confused by this because my previous river piking, on the Hampshire Avon, had been most successful with both sea and freshwater deadbaits. Sessions on the Wye in later years also found deadbaiting to be an excellent prospect but on this part of the Severn, I either used livebaits or had very few runs.

The fish at first proved very naive, falling for simple roaming livebait rigs. The water in the middle section of the arm was not too deep and at normal winter level would typically be five feet or so. A hand-sized roach cast into open water would drift around until taken quite decisively.

Pike that take baits like this so readily have obviously not been heavily fished for. They were beautifully marked fish with many doubles to 17lb coming at first. This happy situation did not last for long though and, as I and others started to catch them regularly, things changed and different tactics had to be used. Instead of the fish freely patrolling the open water they seemed to confine themselves to the vicinity of the flooded bushes of the far bank and a couple of other features that were not apparent at first. An inexperienced angler might not have noticed this and may have carried on fishing, thinking that the pike were not feeding. However, baits legered within a foot or so of the bushes were regularly taken. If the rig fell short, no run came.

Sport was good for a long time but I felt that it could have been better considering the number of pike in there. It was pretty obvious from bringing rigs back that much of the time, the legered baits were lying in the very soft mud on the bottom and were unseen by the pike until they were right on top of them. Mud on the scales and belly of the baits gave this fact away. It probably seems quite obvious to anyone with the benefit of hindsight and all the information available today, but the next move was to paternoster the baits and so put them in full view.

This was easier said than done, because it was actually far more difficult to put a float paternoster rig so close to the bushes than a legered one. Many floats festooned those bushes until every now and again someone would 'borrow' a boat and get them all back! The other problem with paternostering was that the cast was too far, in some of the swims, to be accurate enough and done without killing the bait by continual recasting to get it right.

One thing that we were aware of all those years ago was that paternostering at long range can lead to deep hooking if the popular sunken float method is used. Indication at the rod that shows a 'drop-back' should a pike move towards the rod with a bait, is essential. Many anglers were slow to appreciate this. As the depths there were very predictable, we mainly used surface float rigs and kept a close eye on them.

In those days, we never used overtraces. In fact I do not know of anyone who did. Some anglers fishing that venue had bite-offs through the live-bait catching on the main line above the trace and a pike grabbing it. In years of fishing and catching hundreds and hundreds of pike there on that rig, I never had a bite-off. I am not boasting about it, it is simply a fact worth looking into. The differences in tackle and approach must have been significant. I only used baits up to about five inches long on the paternoster. Bigger baits were always legered. The size of bait mattered not as far as the pike were concerned, as long as it was lively and visible. Many bite-offs came to the 'big bait' boys. Because my baits were small I could get away with one size 6 treble in the lip of the bait. Virtually every one else used the dorsal and pectoral hooking method with two trebles and hence there was twice the likelihood of a hook catching up on the main line. Probably most significantly of all, I kept in constant touch with my tackle. By watching the float carefully, it was possible to tell by the gentle bobbing movement of the float pulling in different directions that it was working correctly. A tangled bait often sees the float twisting around and upending. Those that were bitten off also left rigs out unchecked for hours on end. Generally, I recast an untaken bait after no more than half an hour and in doing so had the chance to check it, as well as being able to cast to an unfished spot. I am still confident today that an overtrace is not necessary if one is fishing correctly but I use one anyway as it is so simple to do and sets a good example to less experienced anglers.

While everyone was casting towards the far bank, few anglers seemed to realize the importance of getting the bait as close to those bushes as possible. Neither did many of them know of the nearbank feature that produced loads of pike – the summer level shelf. The level of the water naturally hid the normal summer bank contours and although this feature was only a slight drop-off of about 15 inches, the pike used it as a patrol route when the area was flooded. It was hard to pin-point exactly where the drop-off was as it was not a constant distance from the margin. Here and there, small sunken bushes and emerging grasses gave an approximate idea of where it might be. Sunken-float-paternostered baits were cast beyond its likely position and inched back until the float showed, indicating the change in depth and hence the drop-off that the pike travelled along. Some very nice bonus fish came from these positions, and in particular from a place where this coincided with the remains of an old lily-bed. Without seeing the water during the summertime, these features would never even have been envisaged. If ever you get to see a pike water at low level, take a few photographs of it for future reference.

Knowing of a backwater full of pike does not mean that you can just turn up on any day and catch a few. It was never as simple as that for me. The height and colour of the water are most important and affect results tremendously.

A PATTERN EMERGES

With levels forever rising and falling as a result of rainfall and tides, no two days were ever the same on this part of the Severn. It was only after fishing there for two winters that the pattern became very clear and I was then able to pick and choose my days and reduce wasted trips.

I had realized that the backwater would be in one of four states; rising, high level, falling or low level. The fishing in each case would be very different and very predictable. In a rising river it was a case of making the most of it before the water coloured up. With a sudden influx of coloured, often icy-cold snow water, the pike would feed well to start with but become progressively dour as they felt the effect of the cold and colour coming in. Very often the residual clear water was pushed to the very top of the arm and it was possible to prolong sport in this area.

When the flood peaked, the water would often be chocolate-brown and sport with the pike was virtually at a standstill. This was often a good time to catch baits and as long as the temperature was not too low some good sport could be had as the roach fed with confidence, knowing that the

pike could not see them so well. In time I learned to avoid these times for pike as the results were but minimal. This was also the time when other anglers flocked there as the main river was unfishable.

Sometimes the flood would last for days and at other times for weeks and this length of time would determine how hard the pike fed afterwards. In a quick rise and fall, the pike would start to feed again in a quite moderate fashion. After prolonged high water things were different. The pike would really be on the move and making up for lost feeding time. It was all a matter of timing, and if one could be the first one there to take advantage, one would be very successful. Ideally, this would be when the colour had almost gone, regardless of the actual level. This was when many of the 100lb plus hauls came out.

When the level did come back to its winter minimum again, several factors came into play. Naturally, timing was important again. With low water conditions, the fishing was fairly easy but, again, the first one there would catch. Some huge bags could be caught at this time but in shallow water it did not go on for long. The pike soon became wary of the sudden disturbance. The water could get so low that feeding pike could not help but give themselves away as they hammered into the huge shoals of prey fish and scattered them everywhere. As the water became really low and clear, the roach soon learned to find sanctuary in the sunken bushes. The pike fishing also slowed right down, with pike usually only showing a flurry of activity at dawn and dusk.

NOCTURNAL FEEDERS

As I packed up and walked away when the river became very low and clear, I often noticed the pike crashing about in the dark. After a little observation it was obvious that in clear, shallow water conditions, the roach shoals only had the confidence to come out into the open as darkness fell or when the light was poor. With so many targets around, the pike obviously found it worth while hunting them at this time. After one such session, I found myself with no livebaits at the end of the day. I seemed to use just as many baits on a poor day by trying out lots of different tactics to catch pike. One particular pike kept striking in the darkness in front of me and I decided to try and catch it on a wobbled bait. Very often, when out of bait, I have caught fish using this tactic. When it gets very cold, as in December, I work the bait extremely slowly by suspending it under a float. In this instance, the wobbled bait was not taken in ten minutes of working it through the swim where the pike was striking.

Pain and pleasure.

Purely as an experiment I decided to cast the hand-sized dead roach high in the air so that it slapped down on the water in the vicinity of the feeding pike. It had to notice that! After several attempts, the line was snatched from my grip as an unseen force grabbed the bait off the surface in the blackness. A fighting mad fourteen-pounder was unhooked using a small mud-stained torch held in my teeth for illumination.

This incident gave me a lot to think about and fishing after dark became a regular practice after a day that had produced very little under low clear conditions. Fish to over 19lb fell to my rods generally on quite small paternostered livebaits. Pike obviously have no trouble at all detecting small movements in pitch black conditions. They feed a lot more than we suspect in the dark when they can attack undercover.

TAKING TO THE BOAT

When the level of the backwater is quite high but the water is not too coloured, it can be frustrating because the adjacent land is so badly flooded that it is difficult to cast accurately to promising areas. This problem was soon solved by taking a small boat down to the river on a trailer. With the water level so high, launching down the normally steep bank was made a lot easier. It was now possible to get right over the swims that I had been casting to and simply lower baits into them. Baits could be dropped right next to the sunken bushes, and with extra water there was no fear of spooking them. Those anglers that never went to this trouble had to put up with mediocre piking and for little real effort I had brilliant sport. In actual fact, the fishing from the boat was actually easier and more pleasant for one main reason. No more *mud*!

There has to be more to fishing than just 'reeling them in' and fishing in such an interesting and picturesque place compounded the pleasure of catching the hundreds of pike I took from this part of the Severn. With so many fish about, other predators were naturally around and I regularly shared swims with kingfishers and mink.

Over a couple of seasons, I came to know that backwater like the back of my hand having seen it at its very best and very worst. Even when it iced over I would go for a drive just to fish in the entrance where it joined the main river.

The sight and sound of the tide rushing in under the ice on one occasion is something that I will never forget. The ice was over a foot thick after a prolonged spell of desperately low temperatures. The unforgiving tide pushed underneath it until it creaked, then it groaned in defiance before opening up with a terrific crack that shook the river valley. An awesome sight and sound! An hour later it subsided and the wickedly low temperature welded it together again as if nothing had happened. Unharnessed energy can be a frightening thing.

A BROADLAND ADVENTURE

Some of my fondest memories are of December. When the weather is bad it is awful but sometimes the evil days are punctuated with marvellously calm and relatively mild ones. It was during such a spell a few years back that I spent one of my many adventures on the Broads with John Watson and a couple of close friends, Andy Hales and Bob Jackson. Fishing alone suits me most times but there is nothing like an interesting and challenging session shared with good friends. By now, most keen pike anglers will have heard of Norfolk's 'Donkey Broad', a private water made famous in John's book *A Piker's Progress*. John made no secret of the fact that we poached it and caught over 300lb of pike that weekend including two different twenty-sevens and a thirty. John described those fabulous days and related what was caught but, intentionally, did not go into detail about how we fished it. As a follow-up to that story I will now do this and the details should give a good indication of how to approach fishing on Broadland.

On a massive complex such as the Broads it is vital to have access to reliable information about the whereabouts of pike as so many areas are either barren or have so few pike present that you

Jacko's seventeen-pounder is dwarfed by a donkey of 27lb 9oz.

Right: 'Watto' and 'Jacko' pause for a chat on Sportsman's Broad.

would be wasting your time fishing them. Naturally, John, as a keen piker and living in Norfolk had done just this. He had discovered the potential of the water by routine exploration and had taken a few nice fish already to 27lb. He had last fished there two weeks previously and had taken a 100lb plus haul including a brace of twenty-five-pounders. Naturally, we had persuaded him to take us there. Without a doubt, this sort of local knowledge is essential when fishing a strange area and saves a lot of hard work. That is not to say that the fishing is easy by any means.

The effort starts long beforehand with preparation. To be fishing on the water for daybreak means getting out of bed nearly two hours earlier. All tackle is prepared the night before and rods are ready made up, parted at the joints and held together with velcro bands. In the half light

you can then be cast in within a few minutes of arriving and you do not miss taking in that often important feeding time.

Bait preparation can be time consuming, so all baits are prepared and packed ready in an insulated bag that is dropped into the freezer ready to lift out in the morning. On this occasion we had made up a supply of buoyant mackerel heads and tails. A net and a large torch makes it easy to scoop livebaits out of the tank. The rucksack or tackle bag is packed with everything except a flask which is made up fresh. With so much done the night before, it is a simple matter to have a quick breakfast and leave promptly. The boat is cleaned out and checked over. Nothing must be left behind as it is too far to go back. Oars, rowlocks, anchors, spare anchor, engine, fuel, engine spares and tools are all loaded in the vehicle ready for the early start. The boat is ready to slip onto the towing hitch and plug in the lighting board.

Launching the boat is one of those jobs that becomes easier the more you do it. For short distances, there is no point tying it on with masses of ropes and knots and as long as one really positive fixing is made to the trailer at the nose-end. A couple of ropes with quick-release slip knots will suffice. A big torch is essential for sorting out the tackle when arriving at the boatyard in the dark and should be carried in the boat in case of emergencies and for use when packing up at the end of the day. The boat is then pushed out into deeper water, the engine started and you are on your way. In the pitch black, you will need to know where you are going, of course! If you are unsure, take an Ordnance Survey map with you. In this instance, we had to motor across a large Broad initially and then find an exit that would put us onto a river. Travelling about a mile down the river, we then had to find the entrance into the Broad that we had planned to fish. Not a trip for the casual piker!

Confronted with a big Broad, possibly of several hundred acres, knowing where to start can be a problem. On the day in question, we had John's previous knowledge to go on and dropped into a likely spot. After an hour, nothing happened even

though we had twelve baits out between the four of us in two boats well spread out. The name of the game in the winter is covering the water until you find fish. Very often there are a lot of pike congregated together and I was used to the routine of searching for a long time before catching. If you do not know about this, you can get despondent and think that the pike are not feeding. When you do drop on them and start catching, the actual fishing is quite easy. John had done very well on this water using deadbaits but livebaits had tended to produce the smaller pike. I always like to use livebaits when I am not catching much and persevered with a roaming live crucian on one rod. After several more moves we had caught very little. If I recall correctly a low double had fallen to a deadbait and I had taken a couple of single figure fish on the livebaits just as John had predicted. The technique used with the deadbaits was to use buoyant ones and twitch them along for a couple of yards every now and again. Half-mackerel were our main baits but generally anything will do.

By early afternoon, after several moves, we finally dropped on pike, hundreds of yards from our original starting point. I cannot remember all the fish that we caught but many doubles followed including three over seventeen to John and Jacko's boat. True to form, the buoyant deads were taking the bulk of the fish and I had one more small fish on the live crucian.

Three 'Donkeys'
Then it happened! Out of the blue a hand-sized, live crucian on my rod was grabbed by a big fish. As it appeared at the side of the boat, we were awe-struck by its bulk. Big pike do not usually do this but that fish just lay there waiting for the net and robbed me of a good fight. It did not matter too much as it was a superb fish! It weighed 27lb 9oz, a personal best and a 'Donkey', the term that John used for a twenty-five-plus fish. The Broad had lived up to its name.

When the light was gone we negotiated our way back in the dark and began the long journey across the broad and along the river to the mooring. Much beer was drunk and a celebration meal

A Broadland 'Donkey' of 27lb 9oz taken on a roaming crucian livebait.

enjoyed. One thing was foremost in our minds: to be back there at daybreak the next morning!

This was easier said than done! We were exhausted from the previous day and some of us had drunk too much beer! I was suffering from a severe stomach pain and certainly not on top form as we slowly inched the boats into position a little after first light. As Andy went to drop our anchor, something made us decide not to. We moved on a hundred yards or so and John and Jacko dropped into the position we had vacated. Within ten minutes we realized our mistake as John bent into a fish. For John to be so excited it must have been something special and I was not at all surprised when he shouted across, 'Thirty pounds, five ounces!'

Then it was Jacko's turn with a nineteen and runs galore followed by many doubles. Jacko was inexplicably broken on a big fish. What a session

this was turning out be be. Suddenly the sport ended and we lost the fish, despite anchoring in different places several times. With only a few hours to go, we decided to spread out and take in unfished water. There was nothing to lose now!

As dusk approached. Andy and I were worn out and I was still not feeling too well. The daunting haul back to the Midlands was forever on my mind and I was not looking forward to it at all. At this point, I noticed that Andy had not recast his third rod. The remaining baits were pretty poor and the fact that we would be packing up soon hardly made him feel like bothering with it. With a little persuasion I tempted him to cast again to my end of the boat where there was a large expanse of water not being covered. The best bait we could muster was a rather ragged-looking small smelt that we would not normally have even considered using.

A December-caught monster of 30lb 10oz.

The unpredictability of piking is part of its appeal. Out of the six baits we had out between us, the most unlikely one was taken – that smelt! Andy bent into the pike and stopped the float from speeding off across the Broad. From the long slow haul in, it was obviously a big fish and, because he was relatively inexperienced, Andy was physically trembling with excitement. As the huge back appeared from the lightly coloured water, panic almost set in but I placed the net between her and the anchor rope and she was ours. I have never seen an angler quite so excited as I set up the camera and flash so that we could take a few photographs. The mind-blowing twenty-seven-pounder, clearly a different one from the one I had caught the day before, was slipped gently back to wreak havoc in the Broadland night ahead. Who would be a bream on 'Donkey Broad'?

These are the moments that we pikers live for. They only come rarely, and that is what makes them so special. To know that with effort and perseverance, they will come from time to time, gives us the strength to keep going, even in the dark days of December.

10 JANUARY – MEN WITH RED FACES

After a gruelling January session on the Broads, I well remember going out afterwards for a meal and a drink in the evening. Four of us sat in the warmth of an open log fire in a Norwich pub, soaking up the heat and living again the events of the day. I looked across at the others and wondered whether my face was the same colour as theirs. Then I remembered an old article I had read as a lad, where different anglers were described by their characteristics. Pikers were the 'men with red faces'. That description had always stayed in my mind and all of a sudden, I knew exactly what the author meant. How many other men with red faces had sat in this very spot over past decades?

Thank goodness that the days at this time of year are short for it can be a month to test the hardest amongst us. No wonder the banks and boatyards are usually deserted. When I look back through some of my old diaries there are some huge gaps where fishing in this month has been brief or non-existent due to extreme weather conditions. Here and there, though, there have been a few red-letter days and as I recall many of the blank sessions in frost and ice I live again the hardships shared with trusted friends. It is no good pretending that it was all fun. Some days were just so awful that we packed up early or were driven to building fires on the bank, so desperate were we for warmth. On many days, the landing net became frozen to the ground and had to be prised away. Even as we netted a pike, the net remained as stiff as a board! Without this suffering though, I am sure that the good times would mean far less. The bad days are best left as brief memories. The good days are made better by the struggle to succeed and many good catches came from nothing more than perseverance.

Brewing up on a cold January morning in the back of the piker's ideal vehicle.

MY FIRST TWENTY

A cold January day in 1972 produced my very first 20lb pike. Although I was used to camping out and sleeping in the back of a van, I had decided that a bit of luxury would do no harm and booked up at the New Queen Inn near the Hampshire Avon at Sopley. This was the third consecutive annual January trip that fellow South Staffordshire Specimen Group member, John Anscombe, and I had made there, having been inspired by writers such as Bill Keal who had whetted our appetites for a river 'twenty'. Modern pike anglers may find it hard to appreciate what a 'twenty' meant in those days. The trout waters were then unheard of and many of the gravel pits that are churning out twenties today were either not dug out then or had not matured enough. We did not have access to many waters and on those where we did, large numbers of pike were killed before they had a chance to reach 20lb. We also know so much more now, not only about tackle and tactics but about what we can catch and where. The advancements in communications combined with increased leisure time have put the odds in the big fish hunter's favour.

The Hampshire Avon was one of the few places in those days with a reputation for turning up big pike. On the first two trips, each lasting three days, I had caught seven pike with five doubles up to 17lb. That would be classed as a mediocre result today, yet then, it was a real breakthrough.

We knew the section of river that we had chosen quite well and had worked out that there were only about three or four swims where we might catch pike. With the weather being cold and windy, we opted to make ourselves comfortable in just one of them, in the shelter of some bushes. The swim was where a shallow run dropped away on a bend into a deep hole that still held plenty of streamer weed despite the low temperatures. I knew from what I had learned before that the pike get behind this weed to shelter from the flow and although the surface looks turbulent and unfishable, a float-fished deadbait anchored with a 1oz lead would hold quite well, although the flow took the float under from time to time.

TACKLE OF A BYGONE ERA

The rods that I was using were as good as one could buy in those days and were 10-foot, thick-walled glass, Aiken S30s. I still have them packed away somewhere. They had hard chrome rings which, incredibly, I used to file out and polish once a year, much to the amusement of my friends! Lined rings like the Fujis and Seymos which we take as standard today were years away. Line, I must admit, even though not of today's superb quality, was not bad and Platil Strong was a popular choice for pike anglers. And yes, I was using an old Gazette bung! Not the huge, fist-sized one but a sensible one about the size of a large egg. This is an item of tackle that comes in for a lot of ridicule nowadays but it had one distinct advantage over a sliding float that is often overlooked and which was particularly important to the river piker. The river piker on the move often has two main tactics. He will be trotting live-baits along the inside and mid-river swims and occasionally wobbling a deadbait, sometimes to reach more distant swims or perhaps to conserve livebaits. When using a split bung, with a peg locking the line in position, it is possible to change from a trotted livebait set-up to a wobbled dead-bait in a matter of seconds. For years I kept one in my pocket for just this purpose but most of mine have long since gone to watery graves.

On the day in question, I had had two runs on herrings in the morning but inexplicably missed them both. I had probably struck a little early considering that the herrings were over a foot long, but they were the smallest that we could get. Call it lack of experience if you like, but I did not even think of cutting them in half! We had, in fact, got into the habit of striking early even then, although it was quite common to see others waiting three or four minutes or even longer before doing so. A third run came around mid-day. I soon got control of the fish and as with all January pike had her beaten after she had made half a dozen stubborn surges away from me. I can still recall how lucky I had been with one treble just in the end of the top jaw and the other outside. We used gags to hold the mouths open in those days and pairs of long-nosed pliers instead of forceps but there really was no need for any complicated surgery on this fish. I was also using a pair of size 1 barbed trebles, something else that thankfully is a thing of the past. While we set up the camera, she was held in a soft, loose-weave sack which was all that was available to us then other than a keepnet. At 20lb 8oz I was overjoyed for, back in Birmingham, I did not know anyone amongst my mates who had caught a bigger one.

A lot of water has passed under the bridge since those days and quite a few anglers have realized the potential of other rivers around the country. The crazy thing about us fishing the Hampshire Avon was the fact that we had two equally good rivers within half the distance of the 140 miles travelled, namely the Wye and the Severn. Remember what I said about 'busy fools'?!

THE WYE IN WINTER

When January has seen stillwaters frozen over I have spent many days river piking simply because it has been the only place I can wet a line. A really ice-cold January day is not ideal for river piking but at least it means that you are in with a chance which you would not get by sitting at home watching the television! If ever there was a time to be a little philosophical about your piking then this is it. If you get no pleasure from the challenge or from just being outdoors then I would recommend that you *do* stay at home in these conditions and get some wallpapering or something else done. I wish I had had the sense to do so at times!

When water temperatures get really low, very often, but not always, livebaits are the only method that will work on these rivers. Even so,

Winter on the Wye.

Sorting baits from my livebait storage tanks.

pike seem reluctant to chase them all over the river as they would normally and they need to be worked slowly and carefully. Let us look at a typical trip along a river like the Wye on such a day. The first thing that you will notice is the colour of the water. If it is very coloured and icy cold I will get back in my car and go home! Should it be clear though, preferably with a slight green tinge, I will be optimistic. Even if the water is rising with melting snow or is carrying ice flows down river, I will be keen as long as it is not colouring up.

By choice, I would prefer the level to be at low winter level as this means that the pike will be well spread out whereas with a heavy flow they will be highly concentrated. This probably contradicts what I have said elsewhere but this is a different situation where I would want to see the pike spread out. On a typical section of the middle and lower Wye, suitable pike swims will be few and far between anyway and a walk of a quarter of a mile between good swims is quite normal. If heavy flows concentrate the pike even more, the number of swims worth fishing is drastically reduced. If you find these swims and can exploit them efficiently without spooking the rest of the pike, you are lucky, but sport for the day can be over very quickly unless you are prepared to walk back to the car and drive to another section of the river. On these days, you are likely to do more walking than piking! Normally the best chance for sport throughout the day is to find the river at a low level.

The first swim you come to might be a deep one near the bank with water further out thundering and churning through. You might see a little streamer weed wavering about to give you some idea what the current in the margins is doing. Casting a bait straight into an unknown swim is asking for trouble. The biggest problem that the Wye piker faces, as he does on other similar rivers, is snagging up. Fast, turbulent rivers are continually scouring trees, bushes and debris from the banksides. They have to end up somewhere and that always seems to be the swim that I intend to cast into!

You might arrive at a swim that you think that you know well but have not fished for a while.

While your back is turned the river seems to deliberately make life difficult and deposits a branch there for you to snag on! January is not a month for having many livebaits either and as you have probably dragged your precious baits the best part of a mile to the swim, the last thing that you want to do is snag up and lose one. It goes without saying, but I will mention it, that you must not leave line and baited hooks down there.

Be bold if you wish and take a chance, but I prefer to take a little time and check the swim out first. It only takes a minute or so but has since saved me a lot of heartache. I simply put on a float and tie a 1oz bomb to the line. Apart from plumbing the swim, I can feel the bomb catching on any snags on the bottom. Naturally, this is done slowly and quietly without spooking fish that will certainly be down there. There might be a shoal of roach or chub in residence, for example, and if they leave the swim, any pike might go with them. Treat the swim as if you were quietly checking it with a view to chub fishing and that should be quiet enough. After plumbing, I usually find that I have one of three options.

Firstly, I hope to find that the swim is clear of major obstructions leaving me free to gently trot a bait through the slack and quickly cover all of the available water. Takes usually come very quickly when doing this. Secondly, if there are snags in evidence, I might be able to trot as far as the snag or alternatively paternoster a livebait to prevent it from reaching the snag. Using the paternoster tactics, I cast into such a position that I can inch the rig back towards me and take in the maximum amount of the swim. Also, in the case of the paternoster, I ensure that the lead link has been knotted to weaken it and if the link snags I can still get the bait back. Finally, in the worst cases, I have decided not to even attempt to cast in for to do so would mean that I would certainly lose everything either while fishing or while playing a pike. There are a couple of swims on the Wye that I know are full of big pike yet I never fish them for this very reason and I admit that I do not know what the answer is. To hook them and keep losing them is just not sensible.

The interesting thing about a river like the Wye is its diversity of swims. In a short length of river it is possible to be confronted with half a dozen very different situations. Further along the river, for example, I might next come to a steady glide, either along the near bank or running away to the middle of the river. For the reasons just mentioned it pays to trot through first of all with a lead supported by a large float just to get a feel for the swim. These swims are just as likely to have a branch sticking up somewhere or other and knowing where they are also helps later when playing a pike. Having worked out depths and positions of snags, try trotting a deadbait first of all if livebaits are in short supply. Having made fine adjustments to depth, play your trump card and put a livebait through the swim. Under normal circumstances, the depth setting is not too critical and pike will rise a long way for a bait, but in icy January water they need to get it right on their noses, as close to the bottom as possible, but this obviously increases the chances of snagging. This is not an easy balance to achieve.

Other types of swim could be described but there is no need, for the point that I am trying to make has been well-emphasized. Each swim needs careful consideration of where the pike might be and of the problems involved. River pike appear from the most unlikely and unexpected places and I have had many a pike, quite big ones too, shoot from right under the bank where I am standing and grab a bait as I have lowered it in front of me to check its action. So search carefully and widely when the water is cold as they may want the bait presented just so.

Although the Wye and Severn start life together in the Welsh hills, by the time that they have reached their lower limits, they are very different in their nature. The lower Wye is very variable in depth with long sections of shallow or turbulent water. The lower Severn, another favourite haunt of mine, is, by contrast, very wide, deep and even-paced, its flow being controlled by huge weirs and locks. Extensive dredging and straightening has gone on in the past when the river was used heavily by commercial traffic and has now

produced a river that is, by contrast to the Wye, very uninteresting. The swims are all much the same, with little depth variation in a given section. The banks are well-lined with bushes and trees which makes trotting tactics difficult and options for piking from the bank very limited indeed. There are some lovely pike waiting to be caught though and the fishing is far more challenging than in most places I have fished.

THE SEVERN IN WINTER

Whereas I would happily wander along the Wye with just one rod, the Severn lends itself to multi-rod tactics. The easiest option along most of the lower length from the bank is the paternostered livebait close to the bank. Fortunately, this works very well and produces a lot of pike when conditions are right. I like to use three rods and paternoster them in adjacent swims. Every quarter of an hour, I move one rod along in a leap-frogging style to the next swim. This gives each bait a fair length of time in a swim, certainly long enough for a resident pike to find it. Normally a take comes very quickly if it is going to come at all but in the really low January temperatures takes often come, if at all, after a longer wait.

The banks can be very treacherous in places, as they can on the Wye where it is tree-lined. This being the case, I simply cast in from the top of the bank and pull the paternostered livebait close to it. The rod is set on rests at the top of the bank in the field and wound down tight to the bait. In this way I only have to struggle up and down the bank when a fish is hooked. As all three rods are easily visible, I often do not take alarms. When you fish in this way, covering great distances, cutting down on as much weight and excessive tackle as possible is a good idea.

Wobbled baits might seem a good idea, but in very cold conditions, when pike want the presentation deep and slow, continual snagging up can drive you to despair! I save this normally deadly tactic for when the pike are more active.

A better way to fish the river more effectively is to use a boat, anchor up behind the bushes and

A typical livebait-caught Severn double taken on a cold still January morning.

trot baits in a way that would be impossible from the bank. I have not found any great advantage in doing this in very cold weather as the pike appear to come very tight to the bank at these times.

TROLLING THE GENTLE RIVERS

On the more sluggish rivers to the east, which are really no more than large canals, a boat has been a positive advantage with pike being covered in a most exciting way. On rivers like the Bure, a boat can be used for trolling baits, both live and dead, and in doing so present baits to a large number of pike. In such rivers where the current is not heavy and turbulent and the depths are fairly predictable, this is a much more practical proposition. The fishing technique is not particularly complicated, but it may appear to be if you have never tried it or have never boat-fished. Proper

organization and carefully thought-out procedures will make the whole business of trolling run more smoothly and it will become very enjoyable! Do it wrong and you will become frustrated and get into a terrible mess at times!

Whether you own your own boat or hire one, the rules are the same and at the end of the day, only you are responsible for checking it over and making sure that it is properly equipped and that everything works. On the Broadland rivers, it is easy to hire a boat and in general they are quite good, being large and stable. Unfortunately, anglers do not look after them and ropes, oars, anchors and rowlocks are often in poor condition. When I hire a boat, I have found it best to take all of my own equipment with me, just in case that which is provided is unsuitable. It may take a few extra minutes in the morning to change things over but at least you are guaranteed a frustration-free day. By the the way, do not

A twenty-two-pounder taken on a trolled roach livebait.

forget to take your own equipment home with you at the end of the day either!

Boats are often dirty, with water in the bottom so I usually take along a few old rags and sponges with me to clean up the seats and remove some of the excess water. This might seem like a lot of bother but there will be enough problems to solve when the fishing starts and it pays to get as comfortable as you can. A tidy boat is usually an efficient one.

If you are only trolling up and down in the area of the boat yard you will probably not bother to use an engine. Should you be travelling much further it is worth considering doing so. This is not for trolling, only to get you quickly to the area in which you intend to troll and to get you back quickly at the end of the day. My preference would always be to use an electric motor, if possible. Petrol motors are heavy, noisy and cause pollution. Unfortunately, electric motors do not

have the range of petrol motors. Also there is the problem of re-charging the battery which is a nuisance if you are away from home for a few days.

You may also consider using a depth finder or fish locator too. As I wrote earlier this is not cheating or a short cut to catching loads of undeserved fish as some suggest. Under any conditions, it is merely an aid that helps the angler to understand more quickly the nature of the water that he is fishing and give him some idea regarding the positioning of fish within the water. To simply gain this knowledge is rewarding in itself and it adds new dimensions of interest to the fishing. You still have to catch them and this is rarely made a great deal easier even after locating them.

When trolling along a river with the fish-finder switched on, you will be amazed at what you will see. I had previously trolled a section of the Bure many times and I had a fairly good knowledge, or so I thought, of depths and snags. The first time I went down the river with a fish finder switched on I was staggered. I knew nothing! In places, the river would suddenly deepen by two feet or so and in other places would be far shallower than I realized. No wonder I snagged up when I set my float to the correct depth in one swim and then proceeded to troll into shallower water a short distance away!

In places, large snags stick up out of the bottom and frequently a large fish, most likely a pike, will be in residence nearby as shown on the fish locator screen. Another interesting thing was the considerable depth variation from one side of the river to the other. I am in no doubt that trolling without a sounder is a positive disadvantage. As the boat and transducer pass over the area first, the angler has a short delay in which to modify his fishing before the bait reaches it. If a very bad snag is denoted, there is time to reel in to avoid it or take evasive action around it. If it is fairly obvious that you are fishing the bait too shallow or too deep you can do something about that too. If you pass over fish it is possible to turn the boat round and troll that area again for another chance.

An important decision to be made long before getting to the boat is how many anglers are to be fishing and how many rods will be used. I prefer to troll alone and use two rods. If someone comes with me, we use one rod each. Using more becomes very tricky, especially when it is windy and when a fish is hooked. Unless you intend to become a master of the art, I would advise you to do the same initially. On a large open water there is more room and hence more scope for multi-rod trolling. By using specially designed rod-rests, baits can be fished further apart. Some can be fished close and others at long-range. I have yet to do this without getting into an enormous mess and prefer a simpler approach. On rivers like the Bure, there will be other anglers trolling and pleasure boats moving up and down the river so there is little room for complex manoeuvres. It is best to keep things simple.

The rig for trolling is quite straight forward. The bait is set on a trace under a float and the float is set to approximately the depth of the water. The bait may be a live fish or a dead one. My preference would always be for a livebait as I find that they catch more pike. If I have to use a deadbait, I prefer a coarse fish as I have had lots of sea baits grabbed and then rejected for reasons of which I am unsure.

The bait is kept down in the water in one of two ways. You can either put a couple of swan shot on the trace next to the swivel or slide a drilled bullet onto the main line above the trace. There are some good bullets available with a soft plastic sleeve inside them to reduce potential damage to the line as they slide up and down. The bullet is useful if you are using a cigar-shaped sliding float as it remains upright all of the time, even if the fish keeps rising high in the water. Whether to use a cigar-shaped float or a simple round polyball is not that important and I have no preference.

When the water is much warmer than it is in January, attention to detail is perhaps not quite so critical. The bait can be set quite high in the water and trolled quite quickly and the pike will rise for it. When the water temperature is very low things are very different and the pike will want the bait to be presented in just the right way if they are to be tempted. The bait must also be at the right depth. In cold water, three feet above the pike's head may be too much. The trolling speed needs to be very slow indeed. They may not be in a chasing mood at low temperatures and might need those vital extra seconds to make up their minds as a bait passes by. For this reason I troll, using the oars, very, very slowly. In fact, the progress of the boat can hardly be detected as it covers just a few yards per minute.

A major problem faced by inexperienced anglers is that the float slides down the line towards the trace and effectively fishes the bait too shallow. This is prevented by fitting a second bead and an elastic-band-type stop-knot below the float or by using a simple device known as a 'trolling-lock' specifically designed for this purpose. As ever I prefer the simple approach and use the stop-knot method. When playing fish up from water deeper than the length of the rod the stop-knot slides easily down the line when the float is wound to the rod tip.

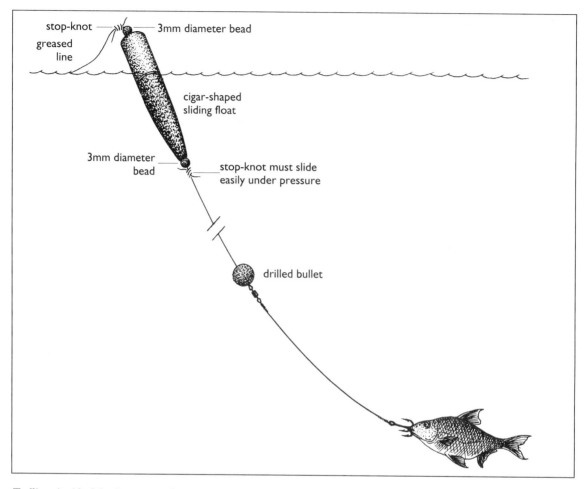

Trolling rig, ideal for deep water. In very deep water, lower the rig carefully to prevent tangling.

As for achieving the correct depth, without a depth-finder or intimate knowledge of the water, it is largely a case of trial and error. On a difficult, cold day when the pike are not too active, leaving things to chance is not a good thing. In water that is less than ten feet deep I will occasionally poke a spare rod over the side and feel for the bottom to get some idea of whether the depth has changed if I have not got a sounder with me. I also tend to err on the cautious side and fish baits a little deeper than need be. I am prepared to risk snagging up occasionally for the benefit of the fact that my bait will be right on the pike's nose if I troll over one. This definitely works, but the snagging up can become very frustrating at times.

If this should happen, you just back up and can normally release the rig from the snag, but you do lose fishing time and disturb the pike if you are not careful.

The line of troll taken is another point to consider. All the advice that you read about regarding features like the mouths of dykes and overhanging bushes rarely works for me. Using a fish finder you will see why because across a river there are dozens of better features that are not visible to the angler created by structures rising from the bottom caused by flood debris.

The best pike-holding feature I ever found was quite obvious after I had thought about it for a while. At times, holiday makers using the riverside chalets will leave keepnets full of fish in the river overnight. They might just as well kill the fish really because when they empty them back, they have no slime left on them and half the scales are missing. As sad as this is, the pike simply get these for their next meal instead of some other poor victims so nothing is lost in that sense. They have just made the pikes' lives a lot easier!

One morning my friends and I arrived at the river to find that our secret supply of livebaits was missing. We had left them in a submerged plastic bin with a soft mesh cover over the top. They will keep for many days like this in cold temperatures and are in first-class condition when we get them out. On this occasion, someone from the boat yard had obviously found them and taken them away. Our efforts to hide them under

a cruiser in a boat shed had obviously not worked. Then I remembered seeing the keepnets and decided to help myself to a few baits. As if in a dawn S.A.S. raid, we inched the boat up to the nets, quietly filled our bins with bait-sized fish and left the bigger ones in there.

Suddenly it dawned on me that these nets must be acting like magnets for pike and later in the morning I decided to go back and troll past them. You get lots of these great ideas when piking and usually nothing much happens, but this time it worked and in spectacular fashion. Andy Hales was rowing and it was my turn to sit with the rods in case a take came. The person doing this has his back to the baits due to the position of the boat's back seat. I never liked this job and would much rather row so that I could watch the

Live baits need care and attention to keep them lively. The bin on the left is fitted with an aerator for transporting them to the water. The bin on the right is fitted with netting, held in position with strong elastic bands. When sunk in the margins, the baits will stay lively all day long.

'Bloody hell!'

floats. All of a sudden havoc broke loose. The chap whose keepnet we had raided earlier was walking to his swim, just as our baits trolled past the scene of the crime. At the same time, there was a great splash behind the boat. One of the rods skidded round momentarily before the line pulled from the elastic-band on the rod butt and the line poured out. Andy sat open mouthed and I instantly turned to see a big pike leave the water holding in its jaws the big roach that I had just hooked on for bait.

When a take does come, the first thing to do is drop the front anchor to hold position otherwise you might be a hundred yards away when you land the fish. In the case of a river with boat traffic like the Bure, you might be put into a difficult position if a cruiser should come past and a pike is towing your boat across the river. With two anglers in the boat it is easy. On your own, it is

still easy as long as you are organized and have the anchor in a convenient position. If possible I like to let out a short rope and play the fish from the back of the boat. With little or no flow on the river, this presents few problems.

Broadland pike rarely fight well in the wintertime but, I am glad to say, this was one of the exceptions and she fought long and hard before she was netted. She gave us many anxious, yet pleasureable, moments as she dashed around the river, clearly visible in the colour-free water. A lot of other pike anglers have commented on the beauty of this 24lb 12oz pike and I am inclined to agree. She was magnificent in colour and shape and caused me to roll around on the bank in jubilation, so pleased was I to catch her under such interesting conditions.

Another tale to tell in a room full of 'men with red faces'!

11 FEBRUARY – BIG OLD GIRLS

Big pike can be caught at any time but the weight of individual pike varies considerably throughout the season. If it is weight that really concerns you, then this month is probably the best chance to set out to catch a pike at its maximum seasonal weight whilst carrying spawn which it will shortly be shedding. It is quite likely that a pike caught at 28lb in October or November could reach the magic 30lb mark by February or March. If you were to leave trying to catch that pike until March it might be a mistake as, apart from the problem of locating and catching it, the spawn, in extreme cases, could have been dropped or the fish might become rather a finnicky feeder during the period leading up to the spawning date.

February weather can be quite variable. The coldness of the previous months can sometimes drag on but often there is a small but noticeable upturn in temperatures. This seems to be enough though to spur the pike into action again after weeks of low activity and I have witnessed some voracious feeding from pike that look so fat that you would not believe that they needed to feed any more. With spawning not too far away, chances are that they will be at or close to the spawning site so it is a good idea to try and locate them there first. However, do not be surprised if, as I have sometimes found, they are miles away. The precise location of these places is not always easy to predict. Rivers are the easiest and pike will be at the entrances to streams and backwaters, if not already in them. They will run into the shallowest of water when the time comes and will also use these places for shelter in a February flood.

On Broads, lakes and reservoirs, there are often incoming shallow dykes, streams and channels and areas of shallower water where pike could be gathering by now. Often it is easy to predict where to find them. One memorable sight I will never forget presented itself as I explored a shallow Channel off Filby Broad. After following lots of false trails you are often not ready for surprises. I certainly was not ready for what was to follow for I was suddenly surrounded by pike of all sizes to over 20lb. I had been as quiet as I was able but had obviously frightened them. First one panicked, then another, until there was a stream of torpedo-like shapes shooting beneath the boat and heading for the open water. An impressive sight indeed. I had found them, but as a result of frightening them my fishing was ruined. I fished the entrance to the channel for hours but never had a run! Reservoirs and pits of even depth and similar features are more difficult to weigh up and it is usually the collective experience of years of pike fishing by many anglers that tells one where the pike are. On many of my local pits, I do not have a clue where the pike spawn but on some, I can at least predict where they will be in February simply from observations made in previous seasons. This information has to be built up as a result of a lot of hard work and there is no point in giving this sort of knowledge away to anyone who is not prepared to go to the same trouble or exchange such details with you.

Enthusiasm and effort are always your main weapons when it comes down to catching pike. The more that you put into your fishing, the more likely you are to find that 10 per cent of luck that is needed to put you in the right place at the right time. You can never predict when this will be and that is what makes the whole business so fascinating for me. The best part about life is its unpredictability.

Unfortunately, as if to make us more appreciative, a proportion of life will be bad news and

Frances Lynch-Smith looking very pleased with her first twenty.

Have you ever said 'My God' to yourself as your legs start to wobble knowing that there is something really special on the end of your line? In a long angling career, this might happen to you once or twice and, for me, this was one of those times. Boy, did this one feel heavy! You could not say that it was fighting hard, it just did not want to come any closer. As the pike twisted and turned, I felt its huge fins catching the line and had that uneasy feeling that it was going to come adrift, as one or two fish caught recently from this water had done.

Closer she came, staying deep in the water, then away she would surge, and nothing short of a broken line would have been the result of trying to stop her. We played this little game for about five minutes or so until suddenly, she came up on top, about 40 yards out, and showed herself with a huge swirl that, for a while, calmed the windswept waves. An enormous pike! Inch by inch, the battle was won and I finally sat on the wet gravel with my prize safely in the folds of the large, soft-bottomed landing net.

Quite a few minutes passed as I savoured a special moment. All I wanted to do for a while was to gaze in wonder at that broad, beautifully camouflaged back, like crazy-paving in several shades of green. You know by now how much I love being on my own at such moments. We actually get to hold these monster-pike in our hands for such a relatively short time. It seems a shame to waste a second of the unique opportunity we have to look at them. With the pike quite safe, recovering in the landing net, where it could come to no harm, I sat and looked at it for a while longer, soaking up the pleasure that it was giving me. The tiny smelt, ragged and almost severed in half, seemed a poor meal for such a brute of a fish!

The weighing procedure was carried out with more than the usual relish and I just could not wipe that smile from my face, which was reddened from endless days in the wind and rain. The weight of the sling was deducted to give a figure of 30lb 13oz!

I cast the badly-mauled bait out again and sat there in the now weakening sunshine. 'Am I still alive?', I asked myself. 'Is it me that this is

hard times – we all take our share. However, there will be some very good times too. After the most devastating episode in my life, the death of my wife Stephanie, I entered an unbelievably exciting run of big pike which was the one thing that pulled me through. If ever Steph could have used her influence up there in heaven and arranged for something special to happen for me, then this would have been it. I still wonder to this day! A few days at the end of February 1989 changed my outlook on life completely.

THIRTIES GALORE

With the roaring south-westerly hitting me full in the face, and the midday sun doing its best to blind me, I looked up at the curve in my rod.

Dave Phillips gets the sling ready to weigh and witness a thirty-pounder for me.

happening to or am I dreaming?' It was certainly no dream for she was still lying there quietly as I set up my camera on the tripod to record the magnificent specimen.

Perhaps you might be thinking that I am going over the top in my description of this moment. Maybe I am, but after a week's piking like that I had just had, I defy anyone not to feel the same way. That fish would have made an unforgettable season for anyone and for most pikers she would probably be the highlight of their career, but the fact was that it was only the *fourth* heaviest pike I had taken in the last week! Luck had taken on a new meaning!

When I got home that night, I phoned John Watson in Norwich and during our conversation I asked if he knew of anyone who had ever taken four thirties in a week before. There are very few pikers who have taken four thirties in a lifetime, came his reply! It suddenly sunk in just what had

happened to me. Anyone who has tried hard for pike for over twenty years deserves a thirty, I believe, but with the thirty-two that I had taken the season before from another water and a couple of recent high twenties, I knew that I had had more than my fair share of good fortune.

It had all started when I found myself with a fortnight's uninterrupted piking which was arranged to coincide with the back end of the season. I will spare you the details but I had had a lousy season after my wife died and I could not get out fishing much at all even if I wanted to. It was painful to drive to work every day knowing that the mild weather must have had the pike feeding like crazy and yet my family commitments meant that I could hardly wet a line. When I finally managed to get the time off to fish, I knew that I just wanted to catch big pike.

My research had led me to find that a gravel pit complex of four pits, in the next county, held half

My rods are stored on racks, ready made up for a quick getaway.

a dozen twenties, a lot of jacks and very little in between. I was not really sure which pit held which pike but, with a bit of investigation, I had a good idea where to start. I had bumped into an old man who told me that he had taken a twenty-one-pounder there on a spinner. Apparently, he had had something grabbing 3lb tench as he reeled them in. He had decided to spin and the twenty-one-pounder was the culprit. The right signals that experience recognizes were coming in to me loud and clear and I had to follow them up. The pits were in part of a disused gravel working and I should not have been in there. Quite a few locals had done the same before me and I understood that the best pike to come out was rumoured to be in the mid-twenties. Due to the stricter policy on bailiffing recently I had to be very discreet.

During the period leading up to my fortnight's holiday, I had taken a few days off work and went

exploring in these pits. I was lucky immediately, taking a 24lb 6oz pike from one pit and an 18lb 10oz pike from another. The twenty-four was only 40 inches long and so had plenty of future potential. I would not want you to think that this sort of luck happens all the time. For every such find, I must have followed up dozens of false trails but in the long term perseverance eventually pays off. I had an idea that the twenty-four was possibly one of the biggest pike, if not the biggest, in there. It was badly marked due to what I later found out was 'red-sore' disease but at the time I mistook it for bad handling.

When my fortnight's fishing started I carried on with the pit that had turned up this pike and was rewarded again with a lovely pike of 20lb 1oz which was unblemished. Like the twenty-four it fell to a float-fished smelt at medium range. The tide was turning in my favour. I always feel that once you get onto something good, you should make the most of it, for it rarely lasts long.

This I did. I returned to the water a couple of days later for another session. I have been fishing long enough now to know that on medium-sized pits, there is every chance of a recapture once you have located pike and I did not mind in the least if one of them would like to grace me with its presence again. I had been through such a lean spell recently that even repeat captures were welcome and especially hard fighting twenties.

I settled into the swim at a quarter to eight and felt much more relaxed than I had done of late. The light rain and the raging westerly wind did not bother me in the least for I had positioned myself where I was sheltered from them. The white-capped waves were crashing against the far bank but, in the lee of a bank of trees, the water in front of me was no more than a little choppy. After fishing some very weedy pits in the area, it was refreshing to find there was very little weed in this one and there was no need to make my baits buoyant. As the pit was still very young, the weed had obviously not yet taken its full hold.

I did not have to wait long for action and at twenty past eight I was away. It was my first run on the pit to a full herring. I have had a soft spot for herrings ever since taking my first twenty on one over twenty years ago. Since then I had had very few decent pike on that bait despite catching a lot with them. As I started to lose line from a fish rapidly heading for the middle of the pit, I had a feeling that things were about to change! If this was one of those other two twenties, why did it not fight like last time?

More line left the spool, in a series of rapid backwinds, and as she kited round, with over 70 yards of line out, I thought it more reminiscent of a battle with a carp than a pike. After a lot of tugging and backwinding, I eased her back and soon she was in sight. As the water was gin clear I could see her quite easily about five feet down. She had a big red mark down the left-hand flank exactly like the twenty-four. I was sure that it was her again. Why had she suddenly decided to fight in this way when previously she had come in rel-

atively easily? Despite her efforts she ended up where I wanted her – in the bottom of my net.

At this point I realized that I had been very lucky indeed for she was just about hooked on one treble, in the flap near the scissors. With the hook just slipping out a second or so, I never managed to look inside that cavernous mouth, which is something I usually like to do. In not doing so, I had missed something quite significant, but I will come to that later. As I lifted the net up the bank to a patch of soft grass covered with wet sacks, I had a strange, uneasy feeling that she seemed a lot heavier. She looked very long and I got the tape measure out to check. She was a full three inches longer than the twenty-four-pounder! It was definitely a different pike and certainly a high twenty. I was almost right – she weighed 31lb 5oz! Words fail to describe my feelings! My life had gone from the ultimate low to the ultimate high and this was a turning point in my recovery from my great personal loss.

After taking my first thirty at the beginning of last season I never expected another one so soon, if ever. The fish had obviously been on the bank before and I later learned that this fish had been out before Christmas at 27lb 12oz but it was to be much later that I discovered this.

Strangely, I went to another water the next day, caught six jacks and thoroughly enjoyed it. That is the way I am! The following day, however, I decided to pursue my run of luck and returned to the 'thirty' pit. Wouldn't you? The weather had not altered much and I settled into the swim I occupied on the previous visit at about the same time. At half past eight, not entirely believing what was happening, I found myself literally re-enacting the previous battle, with another big pike. A full herring was the successful bait again and she took it in almost the same spot as the last one. I was standing there again, backwinding like crazy and with over 70 yards of line out. I thought of Irish pike that I had caught, of river pike and reservoir monsters. None had taken line from me in this fashion. Which of the three enormous pike was it?

From the way the pike pulled, it had to be the thirty, which had fought far more strongly than the other two. Remembering the previous light hookhold, I was a little worried, especially as she seemed to be going on almost unstoppable runs. Running along and using sidestrain I managed to change her direction and she finally kited round towards the bank. In order to quickly gain a lot of line, I followed her with the net and the battle resumed close in. Again I could clearly see the fish battling away, such was the clarity of the pit. I noticed that she did not have the giveaway red mark on her left flank, yet she looked every bit as big! As she came to the net at about the fifth attempt I could see that she was hanging on by one barb on the outside of the jaw. At these times you have to remain calm; every muscle in your body is straining not to panic. The pike will react to the movements around it. In a world where only the fittest survive, do the fish see the landing net as a huge mouth about to swallow them?

I maintained gentle but constant pressure as she inched closer. I kept any other movements to a minimum apart from quietly sliding the net down the steep gravel slope. There was nothing else I could do but allow myself to slide down the loose gravel slope and into the icy water to get the extra reach that I needed. The plan worked, I became completely soaked and the hook fell out as I lifted the net!

Even though the hook had fallen out, I took a good look into the pike's mouth for there was a trace hanging from it. Inside the gut was a small sardine on a small treble and a single and with a length of line trailing. She had recently broken someone! I was not at all surprised for she was probably one of the best fighters I have ever encountered. She was also one of the prettiest and looked as though she had not been out on the bank before. At 43 inches again, she had to be a thirty and she surely was – 31lb 1oz! At ten o'clock I went home. I had had enough excitement for one day and I could not settle down to fish any longer!

Shortly afterwards, while packing up, I had a little disagreement with the bailiff and made a hasty departure, so, the next day I did the sensible thing and kept away. The following morning, however, I just could not get there quickly

enough and was fishing for seven o'clock. This may not seem particularly early but I had a lot of family difficulties at the time and even this was pushing my luck a little. The story now moves into the realms of fantasy for at nine o'clock that morning I was kneeling in the warm sunshine weighing a pike of 30lb 15oz! It turned out to be a repeat capture of the first thirty. It came on a smelt this time, and came in a lot more easily but certainly not without a really good battle and many anxious moments. On this occasion, I had good cause to look down her throat. I do not mind admitting that she had taken the bait right back into her throat despite my early strike and good bite indication; it can and does happen sometimes. When I opened her toothy maw, it was clear that it takes only a couple of seconds for such a thing to happen with a pike of this size if it has the inclination to do so. The sight that greeted me was interesting to say the least. At the opening to the throat, my tiny smelt was neatly fitted in alongside the tail of a tench that must have been in the region of 3lb or so. Only a few days previously I had found a well-chewed 3lb tench floating in the margins. These pike were really on the rampage! In fact, pike all over the country were feeding well, and good fish came out of many other waters during this period.

What else did the pit hold? Were there any other surprises in there for me? I could have gone back the following day but took up an offer to fish a water that was rarely pike fished. I am glad I did. Three runs to buoyant herrings produced three doubles to 17lb 9oz. This brought me back to reality especially when the other anglers there were really impressed with the seventeen which, of course, is a good-sized pike to catch. I never turn my nose up at such fish. After catching three thirties in quick succession it did seem very, very small but it was a beautifully coloured pike all the same. Next morning, however, I was back in the land of monster pike! I had one run on a full herring but the fish came off after a few minutes. It certainly felt heavy! I am sure that you can have too much of a good thing and start to lose perspective. Losing what was obviously a huge fish hardly bothered me at all.

The following morning, in the same swim, my bad luck continued. At ten to eight I dropped a big fish and again at 9.25 p.m. did the same. On each occasion the bait was a herring. By ten thirty I had an awful feeling that I had ruined my chances by losing two pike in the same swim especially as I had taken four different 20lb plus pike from it in a very short time. In a moment's inspiration I had one of those 'nothing to lose' feelings. I gathered all my gear together and headed for the far side of the pit. The sun was catching that bank and I decided to give it an hour and then go home. An hour in the sunshine would be a nice consolation even if I did not get a run!

Things were getting crazy. Within minutes I was away on a smelt and leaning into a heavy fish. I looked skywards at the curve in my rod as the roaring south-westerly hit me full in the face and … I believe this is where I started, isn't it? The 30lb 13oz pike responsible was originally thought to be a different pike but photographs later confirmed it to be the 31lb 1oz fish. I could hardly complain.

February was kind enough to provide me with what will almost certainly be my best-ever catch of pike in a week. I would be amazed if I ever caught four thirties in a whole season again, although I did come close three seasons later when I caught three different ones. I think I have fired my best shots now though and as you get older and worn out, it is more difficult to withstand the physical deprivation and hardship that goes with the dedication necessary.

That is not to say that I shall ever give up. Once piking is in the blood, this cannot happen. As each season passes, I seem to be more and more pleased to catch pike of all sizes and enjoy the search for interesting fishing.

Fortunately, I have also caught a personal best pike that I am pleased with and I realize that I may never better it. We would all like to catch a bigger one, no matter what we catch but I know that I would have to be exceptionally lucky to top the 34lb plus pike caught in 1992. On a different water, February was again the month that brought me the memory of an incredible pike that will stay with me forever.

A PERSONAL BEST PIT MONSTER

Although the heaviest pike that I ever caught came in February, I will admit that I did not wait until then to try for it. This particular fish had fallen to my rods the season before and had taken me a very long time to catch. In actual fact it took me fourteen months to catch it the first time. A chance encounter when exploring a new water brought us together on a warm October morning but, for me, it ended in grief. My first run on this water, coming to a large buoyant fresh smelt, was wound down to and struck in just the same way that I had done thousands of times before. This time I experienced a rush of power that I would not have believed possible from any fish, let alone a pike. It surged away from me in long runs and to try and stop it would certainly have led to a breakage. I back-wound at an alarming rate until the reel spun out of control and ripped the skin off my knuckles. It just went on and on, and away from me in a straight line.

Eventually I ran out of line and with well over 120 yards out I felt the fish weed up or get around a snag of some sort. Slowly I started to get a bit of line back and I imagined setting up the tripod and camera to record a fabulous fish. It was not to be! The fish powered away again and I was down to the knot on the spool! What happened next was unclear but the line suddenly went slack and the badly-strained rod looked sadly straight. It was gone! For a grown man to admit that there were tears in his eyes takes some doing, but there were in mine! My heart was really aching, for this fish was something special. I could not fish any longer and packed up. Almost in a trance, I trudged the mile walk back to my vehicle. It was a nightmare come true.

As soon as I came to my senses, I vowed that if it was the last thing I ever did, I would catch that fish. Through wind, rain, ice and fog, I fished the water that season and caught very little of note. The pit was only about ten years old and held very few pike, as I was to find out.

The following season was gruelling too but occasionally something would happen to keep me going for a little longer when I had almost given up. One vile, cold and windy afternoon, I was winching a mackerel tail in as fast as I could, for I could stand the cold no longer. The rod was violently wrenched from me and the line went slack. The mackerel was gone, so were both trebles and the trace was cut in half and shredded! This pike was now making a fool of me!

On another day, I was so cold that I reeled in and walked to the other side of the pit just so that I could stand on the bank which was catching the warmth of the weak winter sunshine. Unbelievably, as I looked into the water, a monster of a pike had the same idea and lay there soaking up the heat too. Twenty minutes of trying to tempt her with a sardine came to nothing and she eventually sidled away contemptuously into the mares' tails, leaving me more determined than ever to catch her.

Knowing a huge fish was in the water and not being able to catch it made me obsessive. All I ever thought about was that pike. All I ever talked about was that pike. In the end I stopped mentioning it to others as I was sure that no one believed me. Finally a sign came that told me that I must be getting close. I had just taken a pike of 5 to 6lb on a wobbled herring when I was amazed to see that its back end was almost severed off and was bleeding badly. It had very recently been in the jaws of a monster!

That week I went across to Birmingham for the funeral of John Sidley who had been, as mentioned earlier, one of the country's most successful pike anglers. I discussed my obsession with the pit pike with one or two other pike anglers who were at the service. However, I little realized what was going to happen on my next visit. Just an hour or so into the session, in the swim where I had caught the mauled pike, I had a run on a dead perch. That in itself was a major event for runs were rare indeed and usually turned out to be jacks. It was soon very obvious that this was no jack! The fight started as a repeat of that event of fourteen months previously. The fish surged away with immense power but this time I was ready for her. I piled the pressure on to prevent the fish from gaining speed and felt her rise in the water. Still surging forward, she cleared the water

with her head juddering from side to side. The calmness of the icy blue water was shattered as she crashed down. A fight of fights followed. I remember vividly the mixed emotions that ran through me in the ten arm-aching minutes before she was netted. One half of me was jubilant that my moment had come and that my trials were over. The other half of me was realistic and knew that the fish would only be mine when she was in the net. As she came close I almost collapsed when I saw that she was barely hooked by one treble! Finally she did go in the net, begrudgingly, inch by inch, but she went in! When I look at my photographs of this fish, I realize that statistics and weights mean nothing. Whatever she had weighed, she would have been very special to me. For the record she weighed 30lb 10oz. She was long and lean and nowhere near her potential weight. I had caught several thirties before but this was my special fish and the one that I will remember best.

The following season I had to plan my fishing. Should I carry on fishing there now that I had caught the big fish? Realizing the importance of moving on and trying new waters, I decided to give it only minimal time. Apart from the 'monster', there was also a fish of just over 20lb in there which a friend had caught and I had not. Knowing how difficult the big pike had been to catch, I pondered over whether there might be other uncaught monsters in there too.

I fished the water occasionally from the following October but very little was caught. Visits to easier waters this time helped to keep my sanity and my rods bending. The cold months were grim but I always enjoyed just being there. I just got myself comfortable and relaxed, watching the surroundings and enjoying the peace and solitude. I cannot explain the warm inner feeling of contentment that I felt while sitting there waiting for a run. In a harsh, fast-moving world, this was a marvellous escape from reality.

In January, at last, things started to change and I was getting one or two runs. Amazingly, the twenty that I wanted turned up and what a beautiful pike it was too. At 21lb 10oz it took a float-fished smelt at mid-morning. During that same period, I had an incredible stroke of luck on another water that I had decided to start fishing again after hardly bothering with it that season. A pike that I had caught there three years ago at 20lb 1oz, fell to my rods at 30lb 5oz! I was now convinced that I was leading a charmed life. After twenty years of dedication I was finding the crock of gold – time and time again!

When the really cold weather came in late January the pits froze over solid. This was exactly what I had been waiting for. Experienced pike anglers have long recognized the pattern that follows. Bitterly cold weather with regular sub-zero air temperatures and ice on the water slows pike activity right down. That means that when the thaw comes and the water temperature rises sharply, the pike will go on the rampage. This is the time to get on to a difficult water and a time when you are in with a better than average chance of success.

Day after day I did the long trek to follow the progress of the melting ice. Eventually it started to thaw and break up in the area where I was convinced that the majority of the fish were in residence for the winter. They were tightly packed into a large area which was sheltered from the cold, northerly winds and where the weed remained quite dense. Huge numbers of prey fish could be seen dimpling there on a mild day.

As soon as I could cast in, after the ice cleared, I did so. The plan was soon in operation and I took a decent fish on the very first visit after the thaw. I was quite surprised to find that it was the twenty-one-pounder, taking a smelt again in the same spot! I enjoyed looking at her beautiful markings and superb winter condition. This capture also came at mid-morning and, around the same time, I had a jack, a missed run and a dropped bait. The dropped and missed runs were interesting as these had never been a feature of this lightly fished water before. I concluded that one of two things was happening. Possibly the few big pike in the pit were picking up the baits and then dropping them, holding them lightly and showing little interest in them. This occasionally happens just before the spawning period. Alternatively, and more likely, there were large

numbers of jacks in the swim accompanying the big females as they do when spawning is imminent. The baits were quite big relative to the typical jacks of about 2lb in this pit and the jacks rarely take the deadbaits anyway. In either case, it was worth sticking it out a little longer and I returned the next day to see what developed.

As I did the long hike to the pit for the umpteenth time, it crossed my mind that the big pike that I caught there last season might now exceed my previous best of 32lb 12oz. It even crossed my mind that I must be getting close to catching it, but I quickly dismissed such fanciful thinking from my thoughts. I knew that the only way to catch pike was to have baits in the water and that had to be my main concern. I could not put in any more effort as I was almost killing myself already. I could certainly not be considered to be a young man any more and the continual marathon walks with a heavy rucksack, combined with sitting for days on end in freezing cold, damp weather was taking its toll. All I could pray for now was that bit of luck that makes all the difference.

I settled into the swim and sorted my tackle out. I was tying to imagine, as I often do, what I would see if it were possible to observe the fish in front of me. On an apparently featureless water like an open gravel pit, doing this helps me to decide where to position my baits. I take into account the features, where I think the prey fish might be and most importantly, where I have had runs before. On some days, there is something special in the air. What it is I do not know but all seems well and everything just goes like clockwork. This was one of those days! The baits were partially thawed in the margins and cast semi-frozen to be right in amongst the massed shoals of rudd. I had given the pike a good selection of baits to choose from; a smelt, a herring and a dead chub. Baits were fished on the bottom as opposed to being made buoyant as I had noticed that this was producing the runs of late.

From the comfort of my low chair settled in behind some bushes and sheltered from the cold breeze, I started to scan the water and my home-made deadbaiting balsa stick floats which were

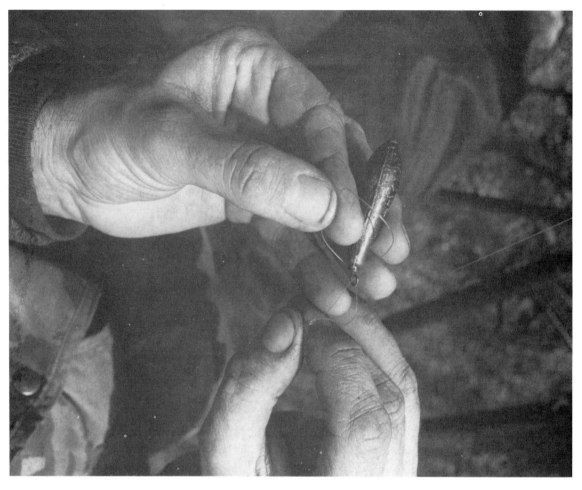

Paternoster and leger leads are attached by simple loops. When walking long distances with made-up rods, I remove them and prevent a lot of frustrating tangles.

lying at an angle of 30 degrees from the surface which was lightly rippled by the wind. At ten to eleven I thought that a run was imminent if the water was to fish to form. It came just as I thought it might and on the left-hand rod with which I had cast a fresh smelt a long way towards an unseen large, broad gravel bar.

When one of those orange-tipped floats stands up, no matter how many times I have seen it before, the excitement is always intense. Only five minutes previously my eye had spotted several large rudd jumping near that float and I had the feeling that they were being hotly pursued by a pair of jaws. I love using smelts because, apart

from the runs you get on them, you can rely on winding down and getting a good hook hold as even if the pike are gripping them at the front of the jaw, the hooks easily rip from the soft flesh and make contact.

This was just another run on a deadbait at first. Although I had set my mind on that big pike it was not necessarily going to come. The excitement comes from the knowledge that every time you strike, this could be the one that you have been waiting for. When the rod bent over and nothing moved, I knew instantly that I was in for ten minutes of hard work. The fight did not start in a spectacular fashion. Ponderous is the word

As soon as I arrive at the water, I put a selection of frozen baits in the margins to start thawing out while I sort out the rest of the tackle.

that comes to mind. The pike was very stubborn and only came to me an inch at a time. All the way, I could feel massive fins bumping the line as she twisted and turned. What a time to be testing a new rod! This was the first fish on the prototype Bruce and Walker Waterwolf MB 2, 2½lb test curve, 12-foot predator rod. It is a powerful rod but with a lovely responsive playing action and this was doubling the pleasure that I was getting. As she came close, I could not see anything. The sun had broken through and its reflection on the water was blinding me.

After several runs close to the bank, I suspected that she was tiring. As I wet the net she

was off. Usually a fish does that only to be stopped within a short distance. Not this one. I had to let her go to avoid a breakage. I am always the first to complain if I do not get a good fight but had reached the stage where enough was enough. I wanted to see that pike in the net! When the float showed itself again, she was right out near the bar where I had first hooked her! The next time she came to the net, the sting had gone from her and it was just a formality to inch her into it. What an awkward fish she was to net. With most of her body over the drawstring, but a large proportion of it left hanging out, I had to make a quick decision as I could not do much more with her colossal weight. I flicked the bait runner in and threw the rod down while at the same time I grabbed the net with both hands and shuffled her in.

There was no doubt in my mind that this was a thirty but I was in no hurry to weigh her. I was at peace with the world and overflowing with a mixture of relief and contentment. It is at times like this that I enjoy the solitude. Piking is a very personal thing for me. I am not really all that interested in what other people are doing or catching. I live in a world of my own and find that the fantasy is often shattered when others are around. As always, when I am alone with a big pike, I sat there for about five minutes, remembering what had happened and re-living it. I took great joy in examining the defeated monster lying quietly and recovering from its encounter with a greater predator – *me*!

I was not entirely sure but I thought that this was the fish that I had caught last year. I ran the tape measure along her first. No wonder she would not go into the net, she was five inches longer that the 42-inch arms! The 32lb Avons bottomed out and I knew I would have to get some help to properly weigh and photograph her. There was still plenty of good daylight left so I sacked her up and when I was sure she was well recovered and safe, I left her and telephoned my friends at the *Angling Times* office.

Back at the water's edge I sat with her, thinking about all the big pike I had been lucky enough to catch and the pleasure that they had given me. I wondered what it was that made intelligent grown men want to devote their very being to catching a huge fish and then let it go! And then do it again!

An hour or so later, Mick Rouse and Dave Phillips trudged round the pit and found me sitting there with a big grin on my face. I think they

What will she weigh? She went 34lb 7oz.

were a little impressed when I slipped the pike out of the sack and we all thought she would be a mid-to-high thirty. We settled for 34lb 7oz even though she looked considerably more. A new personal best for me and my eleventh pike over thirty pounds. Mick, as usual, took some top-class, professional-quality slides and back she went. What a day!

12 MARCH – TREASURE EVERY MINUTE

When March comes around, the hard-working piker is well and truly worn out. Month after month of fighting the elements has taken its toll and really ground him down. This is the time of the year when you might hear him say, 'I'll be glad when the season ends, I have had enough!' He does not really mean that, of course, but he needs someone to say 'Stop' otherwise he would carry on until he did himself some permanent damage. You can become so obsessed with piking that you simply cannot get enough of it and, with the last few days of the season tickling away you treasure every minute, for another season will soon be over. So much has already been done through the winter but it always seems that there is so much more that could be done. If only there were enough time! Something in the air though, tells you that it is nearly all over. Willow buds forming and the occasional burst of warm sunshine hint that spring is not far away. The pike are bursting at the seams with spawn and the old is soon to be replaced by the new.

The piker has a well-earned rest coming and the things that he loves to do will have to remain as memories for a while. He remembers it all as he makes the most of those remaining days. Deadbait floats up-end and slide away, bobbins drop back and bungs shoot under in his mind as he sits and waits for his final runs of the season. Sometimes, just being there provides contentment enough, but time is slipping away fast.

HANDLE WITH CARE

Pike always need careful handling but this is a time of the year when they are particularly vulnerable. In the water they put up little resistance other than a stubborn continual wagging of the tail. On the bank, they often lie quietly, yet the

Pike heavy with spawn, like this 21lb 12oz fish, require delicate handling.

A back-end pike of 20lb 1oz almost bursting with spawn.

Ready-made-up rods are all held together in a bundle by using strong elastic bands. This makes transporting and carrying a lot easier. Holdalls I tend to find too cumbersome and unnecessary.

angler must still be careful. Lulled into a false sense of security by this apparent submission, the angler might not be ready for what often happens and a sudden flip can result in the fish harming itself if appropriate preparations have not been made. It is never a good idea to let pike bounce about or to drop them, but at this time of year it is most critical. As always they should not be left unattended or carried in such a way that they can be dropped.

Throughout this book, I have emphasized careful handling and after a while most anglers can become quite proficient at it. With a friend to help, it is that much easier but you must, if you intend to become a proficient all-round piker, become totally self-sufficient and be able to cope with any situation you may find yourself in when alone. Most of my piking is done alone nowadays,

and I have devised simple procedures that I adhere to rigidly to ensure that all runs smoothly. I can tell you from experience that to veer away from these practices often results in life becoming difficult for myself and endangers the pike. Why is it not done correctly all the time, you might ask? Tiredness, severe weather, difficult slippery banks and cluttered boats are just a few of the things that tempt you to take short cuts and several of these circumstances at once can be a recipe for disaster.

AN AVOIDABLE DISASTER

Last season I fished a Lincolnshire gravel pit that I knew very well. The best fish that I could expect was about 15lb but most were much smaller. I do not always fish for big pike; a lot of my fishing simply involves fishing in places that I find interesting. This water was of particular interest as I was occasionally getting big perch grabbing the pike baits, even buoyant smelts, and you never knew what the next run would bring.

Since my last visit there, the banks had been landscaped and, after recent torrential rain, I had no choice but to fish on a very muddy surface. As I was only twenty yards from my vehicle, I decided to take the minimum of tackle to the water with me to avoid it getting in a muddy state. The rucksack, landing net and other bits and pieces were left behind and I stood by the rods with just a pair of forceps in my pocket. I am quite happy hand landing pike up to about 20lb without a net but I only do it when I intend to unhook them over the water and then drop them straight back. I did not expect a fish here that would be big enough to warrant doing otherwise.

My first fish was a low double. I noticed it had very interesting markings and coloration and so I decided to take a photograph. Against all my principles I carried it up the gently sloping, muddy bank to the vehicle to get a sack to hold it in while I set the tripod up. My hands were caked in mud after trying previously to retrieve my wellington from the boggy bank. I had not got a good grip on the pike and dropped it in the mud. By the time I had sacked it, it was very muddy indeed and so was I. Rather than be sensible and wash I decided to set up the camera with dirty hands, getting tripod, camera and air-release filthy in the process. Again I decided to take a couple of short cuts as I was, by now, realizing what a mess everything was getting into. A quick shot, using a rod on rests to focus on would have to suffice.

Out of the sack came a fairly clean pike, but a very lively one. I managed to hold it still ready for the shot, only to find now that the air-release was just sinking into the mud and I could not depress it effectively with my foot! Losing concentration, I allowed the fish to flip which knocked the rod off the rest. Now I did not know if the shot would be framed or in focus. This meant putting the pike down on the sack while I checked the camera. I folded the sack over it as a precaution. However, I

was on a sloping bank and the pike started to slide out of the sack and into the mud!

I know when I am beaten and so I dropped the pike back into the water before it came to any harm. Totally fed up, I went back to the vehicle for a cup of tea. While I was trying to be a little philosophical about things, the wind blew the tripod over and smashed the camera! At times like this, you feel like throwing everything in the water, and I came very close to it! If only I had kept to my normal procedure!

CORRECT PROCEDURE

What exactly is the proper procedure for landing, unhooking and photographing pike? I have now photographed hundreds of big pike, including six thirties, using a tripod and air-release and I am happy that I can do it quickly and efficiently. I can still remember my early attempts though. However, if I describe how I do it now, you should avoid all the difficulties I have been through.

The landing and unhooking stage is crucial to the effective handling, return and photographing of a big pike. The first task is to land the pike. A strong net with 42-inch arms will land anything you will hook. I prefer to take it to the rod with me, even if I expect to hand-land the pike. When you are having a run of small pike, it is easy to decide not to bother using the net and leave it at the top of the bank. Having the net there gives you a choice and using the net is a much better bet with a very lightly hooked fish that might come off if you do not chin it cleanly first time. A pike in the net gives you a chance to take a breather for a few minutes if the session is hectic whereas a hand-landed pike needs to be dealt with straight away. Most importantly, a run on another rod might come and to be in that position, with a pike already in your hand, leaves you with a difficult decision to make. If it is a jack, you slip it back, but it is different if you should catch a much bigger specimen. If you would like to weigh it, that would involve making it safe first which would mean leaving the other run an unacceptably long time. I prefer to have the net

Daniel and Nicola share the moment as an eighteen-pounder is photographed.

at my side at all times and use it where necessary. If I get a good pike and another rod goes, I leave the first pike in the landing net in the water and land the second by hand. If the third rod goes ... I should be so lucky!

Joking apart though, it is important to deal swiftly with fish caught and get rods quickly back into action. Apart from the benefit to the fish, a run, to me, usually signifies a good chance of another. Ten minutes sorting out the fish and the tackle before casting again might mean that I miss that chance. In fact, if possible, any fish that I intend to weigh or photograph is normally held in the water in the landing net while I re-bait and re-cast and then I deal with it. This is usually a matter of minutes, even if a new trace is needed.

Having landed the pike, it must be unhooked. With this in mind I always ensure that my forceps and a small pair of wire cutters are in my left-hand pocket. Then I do not have to frantically search for them when they are needed and fish can usually be unhooked over the water. Small ones are dropped straight back and never come into contact with the bank. Remember that these are the big fish of tomorrow!

Should it be necessary to take a pike on to the bank, exactly where you will take it should be thought out long before you get a run. Unless the grass is exceptionally soft, you will need to make a soft surface from wet sacks. I normally carry three sacks with me for this purpose just in case I catch fish more quickly that I can photograph them, though this does not happen very often. Be particularly careful where there are thistles and brambles about. On hard surfaces you will need a proper unhooking mat. My E.T. mat also

The thick band of rubber from the end of a balloon makes an ideal run-clip and does not perish or stretch easily as a normal elastic band does.

makes a nice soft seat and back-rest for my low chair when not in use.

BACK-END BONANZAS

In the mild weather that March often brings some of the places where you struggled through the winter suddenly come to life. March has usually been a pretty productive month for me. Where to fish on those valuable last few days can be quite a difficult choice. The fishing is normally pleasant and catches can be tremendous should you find where the pike are congregated ready for spawning. I have lost count of the times in March when I have taken big hauls out of a single swim. As long as the fish are not being

persecuted by lots of other pikers, you can be very successful indeed.

One of the classic examples that comes to mind was a Broadland trip a few years back. Not only does this trip illustrate the sort of catch possible but also emphasizes the importance of location at this time of year.

The adventure started when Bob Jackson and I decided to spend a long weekend with 'Watto'. As usual, we had lots of leads to follow up from John's efforts. One water on the agenda was one of the Broads in the Ormsby/Filby group. I had fished these waters before, taking fish to nearly 19lb but had never managed a really good haul of fish from there. Only fishing it once in a while and after a journey of 170 miles is not really the way to get to grips with a water. It was pleasant fishing all the same.

This trip started in much the same way as any other. Setting out in dense fog in three separate boats, we decided that each of us would explore a different area of the Broad and meet up later to compare notes. This is always a good tactic on a Broad, or any other water, of several hundred acres. After a long row, I decided to drop anchor on a point where the Broad divided into two arms. 'Watto' went up the right-hand arm and Bob disappeared in the mist up the left-hand one.

By mid-day, I had a couple of jacks and 'Watto' came over to report a low double. This was not much to get excited about, so I decided to have a row around, look at the water and catch up with Bob. Even when you are not catching there is something very satisfying about simply being afloat and 'messing about in boats'. At a leisurely pace, I rowed right to the top of the arm, trolling part of the way. All of the time I was wishing that I lived a lot nearer to such a beautiful water!

At last I saw Bob, in the distance, anchored at the mouth of a small shallow bay. As I came closer, I noticed a sack over the side and the smile on his face revealed all. He had found fish! I was green with envy as he rattled off the weights of the pike and the numbers of runs he had had. In an idyllic corner, surrounded by straw-coloured

Norfolk reeds, he had had a boat full of pike including two seventeens, a nineteen and a twenty! The water was barely two feet deep and yet the bay was alive with pike. In the next few hours into darkness, Bob and I added another half dozen fish to over 14lb. Later, Bob revealed that he had followed up a snippet of information we had been given regarding the whereabouts of the pike on this Broad at this time of year. 'Watto' and I had ignored it at our peril!

Next morning naturally found three boats anchored in the bay as we were hoping that the fish would still be there. Even as we moved in, clouds of mud betrayed the pikes' presence and we had runs immediately. Whatever we put out they took it, whether it was a livebait, smelts, mackerel or wobbled baits. On this session, the bigger fish seemed to be holding back when, out of the blue, my mackerel tail, which had been untouched all morning, was taken. I knew it was a good fish but just for a bit of fun I pretended it was a jack. The fooling stopped when it came to the boat with the mackerel swinging about on the trace and the pike clearly just nicked on one barb. One shake of the head and she would be lost. The only thing to do in these situations is to remain completely calm and do everything slowly but firmly. Into the net she went and the hook slipped out as the mesh folded around her. A beautiful

This 22lb 2oz pike took a mackerel tail in a Broadland spawning area only two feet deep.

pike of 22lb 2oz was the icing on the cake from the huge haul from that swim which consisted of fifty-three pike, not to mention another twenty or so that dropped off or were missed.

In mild March weather, catches like these have occurred for myself and friends on many gravel pits, rivers, drains and backwaters. If you can find them and be quiet and careful enough, you can really exploit these situations.

A VERY FAT PIKE

In between bagging up with these big groups of pike in March, I like to spend the odd day in search of a very big pike. Most of these attempts, of course, end in failure. One that did not saw me catching a very fat fish indeed which epitomized the greedy, voracious nature of the pike.

Back in March of 1989, I caught a 40-inch-long pike that weighed 24lb 6oz. That is a good weight for that length but this fish was suffering with red-sore disease. On both sides, it was very red and looked as though it had been dragged across a concrete bank. It also had a growth hanging from its mouth, about as large as a child's hand. It looked dreadful. I doubted whether it had long to live in that state and I did not have much hope for its future. The growth was attached just behind the scissors and I suspected that I could remove it with a little care. The pike lay very still as I cut the growth away with a sharp scalpel blade. I wondered whether I had done the right thing. The amateur surgery had left a hole of about 20 millimetres in diameter, but it was clean and did not bleed. I wished the pike luck as she swam away.

The following September, I had a fish which weighed 23lb 8oz from the same water. It put up the most incredible fight, with the fish jumping clear of the water several times. I thought it might be the same fish but the flanks were quite clean and there was hardly a trace of the hole I had cut! Later I compared photographs and these confirmed that it was the same fish. She was now long and lean but an attractive pike all the same.

During that winter I saw that pike caught several times by various anglers and apart from a few splits to fins, her condition seemed to get better and better. Her shoulders started to thicken up and she even started to put on a few pounds.

In March of 1991, after not fishing the water for quite a while, I decided to fish there again. There were other big fish present that were growing fast, but I was hoping to see the one I had 'operated' on as I felt she had the makings of a very big pike. Her frame was very broad and I felt that, at the rate that she was growing, she would, by now, be well over 28lb and might even nudge the magic thirty mark. An illness stopped me fishing for nearly two weeks, but afterwards I decided to spend three morning sessions at the water. At half past five, in the dark, on the first day, the conditions were typical of the end of the season. Mild, calm air greeted me and as I trudged around the margins to reach the swim, large rudd were flapping about everywhere. The obvious thing to do was to position baits near to them but, despite the promise of better things, only one jack was caught.

When you are after big pike, a quiet session like that should not discourage you if you are confident that you are fishing correctly. It is just a matter of time before things improve. The next morning, the rudd were still there at daybreak and in amongst them, at ten to nine, a fast run on a smelt was missed. Examining the bait revealed that there was a very large tooth mark on the tail. I left, again with little to show for my efforts, but still fired up for another session the following morning.

When you know you are on a good water and you know you are using the right tactics, you need two more ingredients. The first is determination. You never give up if you want something really badly enough. Secondly, you need a little luck every now and again. The two really go hand in hand; by perseverance you make you own luck. On the third morning, problems at home meant that I could not start until half past nine. That meant that I did not see whether the rudd were still in the swim as they always melted away half an hour into daylight. With confidence, however, I put the baits out and, as ever, sat back in anticipation. Barely an hour had passed when the middle float stood straight and jabbed violently and then inched away under the calm surface. For a while, after striking, I was convinced that I was snagged in weed. Nothing moved. Then there was a slight thump on the bent rod and I noticed that the line was kiting to the left. Convinced that I was reeling in a jack, in a huge ball of weed, I was not particularly excited. Time stood still as the great weight inched closer.

When the fish came to the bank I was staggered. The clear, calm water and weak sunshine revealed that I had a monster on the end of my line! Shaking like a leaf, I followed the fish along the bank. I had no choice! When she decided to stop, the netting ritual began. With the wallowing and swirling over, her huge snout, half out of the water, was sliding towards me. In she went but she was so heavy that I had to wait a few minutes to gain a little composure and try to take in what had happened.

Without a doubt, it was my old friend that I had cut the growth from, exactly two years previously. In that time she had not only repaired herself but had grown in length by 2½ inches to 42½

inches. She had also increased in weight as I had predicted but she had far exceeded my hopes by reaching 31lb 9oz. How many specimen rudd had contributed to that enormous bulk? What a fish to end the season with!

Now we have travelled the full circle. The season ends and so does my book. I know that the things that have happened to me could happen to you, should you proceed with the same enthusiasm. I have described many aspects of pike fishing but there are so many more that lack of space prevents me from exploring. I hope you have enjoyed reading this book as much as I have enjoyed writing it. It is not the last word in techniques and tactics. I had no wish to write a dry text book. I hope I have achieved that balance of instruction, entertainment and, above all, inspiration. Pike fishing is what *you* want it to be!

My successes today come from drawing on over twenty years' experience. By sharing some of that experience with you, perhaps I will help you to catch more pike. One thing is for sure. If you enjoy your piking half as much as I do, then you are a very lucky man indeed! Good piking.

This pit pike of 30lb 15oz had the tail of a large tench showing in its throat.

INDEX